INTUITIVE
LEADERSHIP
MASTERY

HOW A CONSCIOUS CEO DOUBLED PROFITS AND HALVED STRESS

By Michael Light

WWIT for you to get amazing results from the tools in this book, expand your business intuition and share it openly in your business?

Table of Contents

Introduction

"We need to make the world safe for creativity and intuition, for it's creativity and intuition that will make the world safe for us." - *Edgar Mitchell, NASA astronaut.*

Overview

Many successful business leaders will tell you that using their intuition or "listening to their gut" helped them get to where they are today. This "killer instinct" helped them make the right decision at the right time, but when asked to quantify this skill, they find it difficult to describe. Instead, they provide vague answers that don't explain their process for other people to follow. This suggests that intuition is something we either have or we don't — a natural born talent — but intuition is actually a skill like any other.

This book shows you how to develop your intuition and gives you the tools to generate more money, results and joy in your business. In this introduction, we're going to explore why it's so important to start developing your intuition (now, more than ever), who I am to tell you about all this, and an overview of how intuition can be put to use in your business.

Why now? The pace of tech and social change has gone up exponentially in the last ten years. Making decisions the old-school, analytical way doesn't work anymore and causes burnout. Business intuition cuts through the complex problem of how to get ahead, without doubling your work hours and sacrificing your health and family.

In the chapters ahead, you will find a hands-on manual, providing the practical tools and exercises needed to develop your business intuition skills, including:

- Powerful Visualization Methods
- WWIT (What Would It Take) Tool
- Decision Journaling
- Negativity and Self-Sabotage Clearing

The application of these tools in your business include:

- Business and Team Vision
- Hiring, Managing, Firing
- Marketing and Sales
- Decision-Making
- Reducing Stress

As we go on, we'll look at many intuition tools — ranging from basic to advanced — that you can use in your business. While these tools were developed over many years by intuition practitioners for use in all parts of life, I have focused on applying the methods to my business and my clients' businesses. They can be used for faster hiring, increasing sales and creating more cohesive teams in your company, among many other uses.

Once you've got a handle on the tools, we'll look at how you can "10X" your business intuition. One of the common misconceptions people have is that intuition is a fixed part of who you are — that you're born with some level of intuition, and that's all you're going to get. Not true. Like developing other parts of your mind and body, you can 'go to the gym' for business intuition and become a "super intuitive" leader.

Finally, we'll look at some resources you can use to develop your intuition even further, and how you can start teaching your staff how to use their intuition to improve your business. As you progress to this stage, you'll see intuition start to cause a chain reaction of growth and development in your company.

To get started, let's talk about why intuition is important in your business, now more than ever.

Why now?

Intuition has a history as long as humanity's. We've been listening to our gut (or ignoring it at our peril) in life and business for thousands of years. We've seen endless examples of intuition paying off, and just as many examples of people paying the price when they don't listen to their intuition. In 44 B.C., Calpurnia, wife of Emperor Julius Caesar, foresaw his assassination and begged him not to go to the Senate. Caesar didn't listen. A dozen stab wounds and three famous last words later, he was dead.

CEO Mandi Hill Ellefson started using these tools last year and says:

> "Since I've committed to massively improving my intuition, great things have happened for me. I notice when I'm stuck and that I can get out quick, realize the source is something outside of myself and unplug from it and make better decisions."

In today's world, intuition is even more important than ever. This comes down to four factors:

1) Logic alone is no longer enough.

This is particularly true when other human beings are involved, because 'people issues' have so much data. For example, in hiring, there's an enormous quantity of information that you could take in to hire the right person. But if you rely on spreadsheets and analyze it all logically, you'd take six months to hire anyone. By that time, one of your competitors will probably have hired all the good candidates and you're left with all the crap candidates, which is how many traditional businesses typically operate. They take weeks to hire, so you can get ahead of them by hiring quicker.

2) Spiritual shift.

Right now there's a raise in consciousness and a spiritual shift that's occurring, and that's occurring in every area of life, and business is part of that.

> "There's a shift happening in humanity, a shift in consciousness, happening now because it has to happen now." — Eckhart Tolle

There is a move from fear to love, from separation to oneness, from unconsciousness to awareness. The increasing popularity of yoga is an example of this. The desire of workers to have jobs with meaning as well as money is another.

3) Competitive edge.

You can choose to ride this wave of change and this gives you a competitive edge. If you can do things quicker and get more correct decisions, better hiring, better sales with less effort, you're going to do better than other companies that are doing it the old way.

4) Information overload.

There is a tremendous amount of information coming into our orbit every day now. The speed of business has increased significantly in the last few years, and you can't make decisions in your business purely by logic and expect to keep up with the speed of everything coming in.

The singularity problem

Part of the reason for the increase in the speed in business is the fact that there's so much change in technology in many different areas happening now. And it is accelerating. This is referred to as "The Singularity" because the graph of change looks like it goes vertical as a singular function such a $1/x$ at x=0.

It's not just computers that are changing faster each year. It's nanotech, gene tech, Artificial Intelligence, Virtual Reality, Space Tech and more. The rate of change is reaching the exponential hockey stick moment. People tend to think linearly — we think, "If it went up so much in the last ten years, it's only going to go up that much in the next ten years," but really, the curve is going up exponentially. You think technology is crazy now? Just wait a year or two. It's going to get a lot more crazy.

Why business intuition?

> "Who knew that intuition could be so practical? It takes the pressure off having to 'figure out' the 'right answer' — instead, use intuition to guide you. It feels easy and effortless... and it works." - Amanda Cook, CEO of Wellpreneur

One of the problems in business is that we treat our mind as the one in charge. The intuition is just hanging around to be checked in with occasionally. Let's change that. Both the mind and the intuition are just tools we can use. We are spiritual beings with a body having human experience. The mind is there as a tool to be used. Logic and rationality are there as a tool. They're not here to run the show.

> *"The intuitive mind is a sacred gift and the rational mind is a faithful servant." - Albert Einstein*

How I got into business intuition

Who am I? Why am I here telling you about business intuition? I have been in business for over 27 years. I run a custom software company, I have organized conferences for thousands of people, and now I provide intuition coaching to CEOs and leaders.

This coaching helps CEOs to dramatically increase their business intuition so that they can grow their business faster with less stress (without burning out by adding more work hours trying to add another "solution").

In a 1,000 member international entrepreneur community, I am known as "Mr. WWIT" (What Would It Take). WWIT is a method I use to access intuition to solve business problems fast, and you'll learn more about that in the next chapter.

Logical time

At school I did a math degree — you can't get a bit more rational than that! I used to run my business very logically and organized to-do lists, pros and cons, and many spreadsheets. Then in 2000 I started doing spiritual-intuition training and applied it to my business.

It has been 15 years since I stopped only using my logical brain to run my businesses and stepped up my intuition to help me make faster and better decisions.

More recently I have done business coaching to help CEOs reach their goals 4x faster than before. Here is what one of my clients had to say:

> *"I'm working on things that are more fun, more exciting and more enriching for me...from a personal perspective, but also from a career standpoint. I have to say, this is surprising for me because 2016 will mark the ninth year of me running my business. I was actually looking to exit my business and to try something completely new, different and more exciting. But after working with Michael for the past three months, I realized that I didn't have the right framework to reach my goals." - Dustin Overbeck, CEO of Town Web*

Before this intuitive shift, I wasn't fully happy

I used to worry about making the right decisions. I would work long hours, sometimes drinking beer to keep going late at night. I would create complex pro/con spreadsheets but still end up hiring people who were not a great fit for my company, who stole from me and messed up projects.

I tried to put on a smiling face for my staff and clients, but it was a sham.

Underneath it all, I was in long-term, low-grade depression.

My business did not turn me on anymore. I was a complaining expert. The passion had gone from my life.

I would go out drinking on weekends to try to add some joy into my life. But that didn't really work.

And at home, I would overeat to stuff down the negative emotions, gaining 30 pounds in a few short years.

Honesty in 2000

In 2000 I joined a truth-telling group to try to save a 7-year relationship. The romantic relationship died, but through truth and communication skills, we expressed what we had not been able to do in the years before and remain friends.

Then I went to a nine-day honesty retreat and started bringing better communication skills into work.

I came out at work and in public as transgendered and bisexual, because living my truth became more important to me that obeying other people's judgments about me.

I went to hundreds of conferences and workshops on personal growth, spirit and magic, and gradually my intuition started to increase.

I added handwriting analysis to my hiring process, and cut out all the bad hires I had made before.

As I went further down the rabbit hole of intuition and spirit, I learned that we create our own reality. Realizing that I had created the mess in my business was a bummer for a while... until I realized now I had the skills to recreate it any way I wanted.

Yoga and health

After a car accident in 2001, I started doing yoga regularly. Soon I had quit drinking and had cleaned up my diet, had started meditation and was going to ten-day yoga retreats twice a year.

Then I did yoga teacher training. More as a way for deeper spiritual growth than to teach, but boy, did it kick my butt and wake up my intuition.

Listening to my intuition

In 2010 I started to get strong messages from my intuition that I should go to the Andes. I didn't know anyone there, why I should go or what the heck I would do there. I was frighted out of my mind, but once I arrived in the mountains of La Paz, I knew I had made the right decision.

I felt more peaceful than I had in years and easily met other yogis and spiritual workers there. My software business even ran better than it did when I was in the US.

Later, I moved to Cusco, Peru, where there are even more healers and other spiritual people. I continue to live there six months of the year, and spend the rest traveling in Europe, Asia and the US in the other months, for conferences, entrepreneur events, and the simple joy of traveling.

The idea for this book came from my intuition. In many ways, instead of me writing the book, the book wrote through me.

What areas can you use intuition in your business?

What areas can you use intuition in your business? All of them.

- Vision (the vision of your business, how you create the vision of your business, how you communicate it effectively to your employees, to your clients, to your vendors, the public)
- Hiring, managing, firing
- Marketing and sales
- Accounting and legal
- IT
- Deals and business sales
- Your health and happiness

That final item — health and happiness. This, too, is a business area, because usually, the reason we are in business is ultimately to be happier. Why do we go through all of the work to have a business? Sure, to earn money, to have status, to be successful, perhaps to change the world. But why do you want to do all those things? The bottom line is to be happy, so why not get the happy part quicker along with the rest through taking care of both your physical and emotional health.

Intuition ups your game

Business intuition works in all work areas. — military, legal, medical, manufacturing, farming, IT and more. Let's look at two of these.

The stereotype is that the military is super rational, organized. Everyone's following orders. But as soon as troops get into battle, you get what they call "the fog of war." The fog is too much information, chaos and confusion. That is when intuition becomes invaluable. Many soldiers can tell stories of when intuition saved them. The same is true in any fast-moving business situation.

Example: Staff Sgt. Martin Richburg, whose intuition told him something was odd about a man at an Iraqi Internet cafe. He acted on his hunch and saved 17 cafe patrons from the bomb the man had just planted there.

In another incident in Iraq, a soldier's intuition and situational awareness was a lifesaver:

> *"In hindsight, some of the soldiers acknowledge their 'spidey sense' was tingling. It was quiet that day. Possibly too quiet, as the platoon motored through ... Thanks to the awareness and quick actions of a 99th Regional Readiness Command (RRC) Soldier, however, no one was seriously injured by the [IED] attack--and he did this all while communicating with his wife on a cell phone..."* - Chris Coleman in the Army Reserve Magazine

The US Navy created a program called "Enhancing Intuitive Decision-Making Through Implicit Learning" which investigated how members of the military could be trained to improve their "sixth sense," or intuitive ability, during combat and other missions.

There's another military concept that applies to business — the OODA loop. (OODA = Observe, Orient, Decide, and Act, developed by military strategist and United States Air Force Colonel John Boyd.)

Soldiers work to get inside the opponent's OODA loop. The only way to do that fast enough is to use your intuition. You can't plan everything out and look at all the possibilities, because if you do that, your opponent will have gotten inside your loop and you'll be dead.

Business failure does not result in death, but if your opponent can maneuver faster than you using intuition, and get inside your decision loop, then your business will be toast.

Law may seem to be a very logical work field. But lawyers use intuition, too. Good trial attorneys are able to go for the jugular with their opponent, and they may not be able to explain it at the time. They can probably explain it later. But, again, attorneys like to be seen as being very logical or analytical, so they don't always talk openly about using their intuition, even though the best have great people instincts. They know when a witness is lying and they need to push them, or when not to pursue a line of questioning, what the mood of the jury is.

The same is true of top business leaders in a tense deal negotiation. Intuition tools gives you that extra edge.

The future of Business Intuition

I have a dream about business intuition.

Today if you ask any CEO "Does your business use spreadsheets?" 99% say "Yes." If you met an entrepreneur and they said, "I'm not going to use spreadsheets, they're kind of weird, it's a bit too newfangled for me," you would think it didn't make sense.

In a few years, the same will be true of using intuition tools openly in your business. It will be a no-brainer to use them because they work and make your life easier.

By reading this book, you are on the cutting-edge of business leadership. You have the opportunity to get ahead of a lot of other leaders and to live a life that is more joyful and successful that you thought possible.

Homeplay

Homeplay is similar to homework except you can play and have fun with it. Each chapter ends with some suggested homeplay exercises that can make your learning of business intuition faster.

- How have you used intuition in your business up till now?

- How would you like to be using it?

Bonus Materials

You can find bonus spreadsheets, audios and videos for the book at www.intuitiveleadershipmastery.com/bonus/

CHAPTER 1

Intuition Toolkit

"I rely far more on gut instinct than researching huge amounts of statistics." - *Richard Branson, CEO Virgin Group*

Introduction

In this chapter, we introduce some powerful intuition tools that you can immediately apply to increase your business profits and reduce your stress. We start with WWIT (What Would It Take) and its variants. Then we learn how to TLC (To the Light, Connect) and how this can improve your business. Finally, we learn about the Office of the Mind and your Spiritual Advisory Board.

WWIT

WWIT (What Would It Take) is a powerful business intuition tool. It lets you solve problems and delete worries fast. Don't be deceived by its simplicity.

For example, if you ask, "What would it take to attract ideal clients?" or "What would it take to add 10 percent to my income this year?"

then immediately you start thinking of things that will solve that problem.

Just stop reading for a few seconds and try it out yourself on a current business problem that you have. Come back to this page when you're ready.

I imagine you got some ideas immediately. If not, don't worry. I will explain later how to use it in more detail to get the most results.

To start, let's explain WWIT and how you use it in your life and business.

I first learned WWIT from Christie Marie Sheldon a few years ago in her Unlimited Abundance course. I have subsequently Googled to find where WWIT came from and found that the concept is in the public domain.

WWIT is a way to shift the focus of your mind away from the problem and onto solutions. I believe it also activates our intuition and subconscious to jump forward to finding big answers, rather than working hard to figure out solutions made up of logical steps.

The phrasing of WWIT is interesting as it focuses on actions to achieve the goal in mind (the **Take** part), and the **Would** part focuses on the idea that solutions are possible.

It is powerful because instead of focusing on the problem and worrying about it, you are now focusing your brain on finding solutions. It's sort of like putting something into Google — you enter your question into the search bar, and then Google goes off to make the search. You put WWIT into your brain with a question, and your brain starts searching for the answer (even if you don't think you know of any solutions right now).

On a spiritual level, WWIT is a clearing question. It helps to remove or clear up anything that is in the way of you getting what you want. Perhaps you have resistance to achieving your goal or you self-sabotage in this area of your business. Asking WWIT starts clearing this and may also bring to your conscious mind specific resistance or beliefs for you to clear.

Ask WWIT, then get really quiet and tune in to ask yourself, "What would it take for me to find my ideal client?" You can answer either in your mind, out loud or simply write it down.

To get good, actionable answers to the "WWIT to find my ideal client" question, you must first have a clear idea of who your ideal client is. Often, part of the problem is that you're not clear about some critical part of your question.

This example — finding ideal clients — is a huge problem that I see in businesses all the time. If you're attracting clients who only stay for a few months, are painful to deal with or don't have enough money, that would suggest to me that they're not ideal for you. Clarity is critical — on both a practical level and a spiritual level, how can you expect the universe or other people to give you what you want if you don't know what that is? The WWIT question helps you to develop the clarity you need in order to find the right people to work with.

I asked attendees at a workshop to share how they had used WWIT. Here is what one said:

> "I did What Would it Take for me to get to $X amount extra revenue in my business. I realized I needed another four clients. I wasn't sure I would be able to get that many leads to go ahead, but everyone I spoke to said yes. This made an

extra $4K per month, $48K a year. Just from sitting down and doing What Would it Take for five minutes."

That is an impressive rate of return!

WWIT Modifying Words

I use WWIT in all parts of my business and life.

Whenever I have a goal, I ask WWIT to achieve this goal with ease and joy? (Or whatever **modifying words** I want to add to the goal to get it in the way I want.) For example, "WWIT to win this proposal with ease and joy this week?"

When I have a problem, I ask WWIT to solve it *with ease*? (Again, add whatever modifiers to solve the problem you're dealing with.) For example, "WWIT to have this employee work reliably in the future?"

I use ease and joy as WWIT modifiers because I prefer to create business results that way.

I am less stressed this way, compared to the time in my life when I used to create results with struggle and pain. (This is a common hidden belief among business people — that good results require struggle and pain.) Using these WWIT modifiers helps me to avoid falling into that trap now.

Another common WWIT modifier is a time based one. For example, "WWIT to have an extra $X in my business bank account this month?"

I often use *now* as a time modifier. For example, "WWIT to hire an ideal developer now?"

This gets my mind focusing on ideas that produce good results quickly, rather than ideas that might pay off in a year's time.

You can add the modifier "or something better" to open you up to other better possibilities, even ones that you don't know consciously before you ask. For example, "WWIT to have a successful landing page, or something better?" You may come up with ideas for hiring an outstanding landing page designer or perhaps you come up with an even better method for reaching your ideal clients without a landing page.

Nested WWITs

So you now know basic WWIT (What Would It Take) and modified WWIT. One more powerful WWIT method is Nested WWITs.

Suppose that you are doing a What Would It Take for something you want to create in your business. For example, let's say you're looking to choose the best marketing channel on which to focus your efforts.

Start by asking yourself:

- What would it take to find the best marketing channel to focus on in order to grow my business? Ask yourself the question and see what inspiration you get in the silence after the WWIT question.

Perhaps you hear "Blogging" from your intuition. So, using nested WWITs, you ask another WWIT question:

- What would it take to blog successfully for this business?

That is WWIT nesting. You've got an answer, but you're not quite clear what to do with it or how to get there. So you ask another What Would It Take. Then you may go down a third level or a fourth level.

This helps you get results faster because sometimes your intuition will give you answers, and you think to yourself "Ok, but how am I going to do *that*?" That is where you keep asking WWITs until you are clear what practical steps you can take *now*.

To recap **Nested WWITs**:

- Ask the first WWIT and come up with an action that will get you to the goal.
  - Then ask another level of WWIT on that sub-goal.
    - Repeating down the sub-sub-..... goals
- Until you come to an action that you can do now.

Here is another complete example to help you get this idea more fully:

- WWIT to generate an extra $1000 this week?
  - Get three new customers
    - WWIT to get three new customers this week?
- Send out a mass email to my prospect list with an offer

Multi-dimensional WWITs

How long does WWIT take to manifest? That depends on how much resistance you have to manifesting it.

> *"When people ask us how long does it take for something to manifest, we say, 'It takes as long as it takes you to release the resistance. Could be 30 years, could be 40 years, could be 50 years, could be a week. Could be tomorrow afternoon.'"* — Abraham

To release resistance faster, you can ask yourself several WWITs for your goal in different time periods.

- WWIT for your result to manifest in 30 years?
- WWIT for your result to manifest in 40 years?
- WWIT for your result to manifest in 50 years?
- WWIT for your result to manifest in 1 year?
- WWIT for your result to manifest in 3 months?
- WWIT for your result to manifest in 1 month?
- WWIT for your result to manifest in 1 week?
- WWIT for your result to manifest in 1 day?
- WWIT for your result to manifest now?

By playing with the time component, you can release different aspects of the resistance you have to manifesting this goal.

Similarly, if you want to generate more profit in your business, then use multiple WWITs to generate different amounts. Even if you have a particular amount in mind, the other amounts will loosen up your resistance and give you new inspired actions. Pick the amounts that come to your intuition so they are somewhat random.

For example:

- WWIT to generate an additional $10k in profit this month?
- WWIT to generate an additional $1k in profit this month?
- WWIT to generate an additional $177 in profit this month?
- WWIT to generate an additional $357k in profit this month?

- WWIT to generate an additional $1 in profit this month?

How WWIT works

There are several aspects to how WWIT works and how you can use it for maximum effect.

First, WWIT works a lot better when you TLC (To the Light, Connect) before you use it, and I'll explain how to TLC in detail below. By doing TLC, you will get much more inspiration and idea flow, faster than when you are in a lower vibrational state. By lower vibration, I specifically mean one of the lower emotions such as shame, guilt, fear from the full Hawkins scale further down in this chapter. Any state below love is less good for getting inspired ideas from WWIT.

Secondly, you use WWIT to get ideas, to get inspired actions. You are asking your intuition, your higher self, your angels and guides for answers. At the same time, it puts the mind into a solution mindset — instead of saying, "I'm worried about how to solve this problem," which is a way to close down your mind, you're opening it up with a WWIT question. You're telling your brain: "Give me the solutions!"

Brains are trained to go after whatever you tell them to go after. If you ask your brain to answer "What Would It Take to…" it goes off on a search, just like Google, to come up with the best result.

Thirdly, when you work through a WWIT, you are clearing spiritual blocks that are in the way of you getting what you want (particularly when you bring in light at the same time using TLC). So if you are looking to add $4,000 per month in revenue to your business, you might have previously had concerns about how much hassle it was going to cause, whether you would have to hire someone to handle the extra work and so on, but when you do this What Would It Take, it helps clear out that stuff. Typically that stuff has come from childhood and your early programming, but we'll get back to that later on in Chapter 6 with the Youngest Age Pattern Recycling tool.

Here is what entrepreneur Amanda Cook had to say about her WWIT experience:

> "I wanted to share with you how I've been using What Would It Take In My Business. Michael taught me about using the question, 'What would it take' recently, and as soon as I tried it, I just felt really light and spacious. Sometimes I have this tendency to get stuck in my head trying to reason a problem out. But for some decisions, especially when you're trying to tune in to your intuition and your gut, thinking about it too much just complicates things.
>
> That's why I really have enjoyed having WWIT in my toolbox. Being able to ask 'what would it take?' means that now when I feel stuck on a business problem, or like something is going to be too hard to do, I can just ask myself, 'Well, what would it take for that to feel easy?' Or, 'What would it take to reach 100 new people with this product?' Or, 'What would it take to make this profitable?'
>
> When you ask that question and then sit back and see what bubbles up, it's a much more empowering answer that comes back. For me, What Would It Take has been really freeing. It takes the pressure off — I don't feel like I need to figure it all out in my head anymore. I can just ask the question and then see what comes up from inside me. I'm really thankful that I learned this question from Michael."

Another entrepreneur Elisa wrote about WWIT:

> *"I've been practicing WWIT for a while now and have incorporated this into my journalling. It's liberating! Not only that, it shifts my focus to the solutions instead of problem — it is also emotionally liberating. It's an act of 'let go and let God,' and setting an intention at the same time while allowing myself to tune in to the solutions. Even if the answer isn't obvious now, it doesn't bother me as much as it would have in the past, as I know that I've asked for help."*

WWIT in Projects/Goals

I will end with some WWITs you can use to make your company goals even more successful.

- What are three big projects that you are going to focus on this year?
  - WWIT for each to be successful, profitable and joyful?
- What do you need help with?
  - WWIT to get that help?
- What's one problem that you want to totally solve this year?
  - WWIT to do that easily?
- What do you wish you would have done differently last year?
  - WWIT to change that with ease and grace?
- This year will be your most successful year if you _____.
  - WWIT to do that?

How to Delete Business Worry with WWIT

Are you spending lots of time and energy worrying about your business? I know I used to. Worrying if a sale will close this month, worrying if a new hire will work out, worrying if a loan will be approved... it's exhausting, and saps the energy and creativity you bring to your work.

Here is how you can immediately delete worry from your business and gain back that lost time and energy.

The next time you notice yourself worrying about something, substitute WWIT! It is that easy to do... The hard part is remembering to do it.

Examples

- I am worried we won't make our quarterly revenue goal. → WWIT to make our quarterly revenue goal easily and with joy?

- I am worried that Bob (VP of Marketing) is not working well with his team. → WWIT for Bob to be easily working well with his team?

- I am worried that project X won't launch successfully. → WWIT for project X to launch successfully, profitably and joyfully?

Notice that I added in some modifying extra words in the WWIT question, such as joy and profits. You can add in whatever you want to create as the opposite of your worries.

By using WWIT, you will start focusing on solutions instead of worrying about the problem. You will start taking actions and building energy instead of losing it.

TLC

The most important intuition tool is TLC. TLC stands for To the Light, Connect. (It also is an abbreviation for Tender Loving Care, which is what you are doing for yourself when you use this tool). TLC helps you perform at a higher level in your business and makes your WWITs more powerful.

Here is how to TLC:

- Put both feet on the ground. Why? Because if you have both feet on the ground, you ground better and connect to the Earth energy better in the later steps.

- Close your eyes for a moment and take a breath.

- Take your consciousness up like your mind is in an elevator ... go up a few thousand miles up into space where it's all truth, light, and beauty. There's none of this human crap up there.

- Bring this light down from above...
  - through the top of your head
  - through your throat, so you can speak your truth
  - through your heart, so you can feel your truth, and experience the love in your business
  - through your stomach, so you are powerfully expressing yourself through your business
  - through your abdomen, so you can clear out any abuse or trauma you have with money or business issues
  - down through your hips and legs so you're grounded in your business.

- Take this energy and your consciousness down through the room you are in, down through the Earth, down, down to the center of the Earth.

- In the center of the Earth, connect with the energy of Mother Earth, of unconditional love, acceptance, and understanding.

- Then bring the energy back up through the Earth, through your feet, your knees, your legs, your tummy, your heart, your head.

- Now you've got light coming from above and light coming from below. It's like a divided highway, both flowing at the same time.

- Finally, expand your heart out...
  - as big as the room you are in,
  - as big as the building,
  - as big as the city,
  - as big as the country,
  - across the continent,
  - the planet,
  - the solar system,
  - galaxy,
  - and universe.

Now you are connected to the light above and below, and you've expanded your energy to be as big as the universe.

Notice how you feel.
Slowly open your eyes.

The first time you are led through that process, it usually takes about a minute. Once you get used to doing TLC, you will be able to do it with two breaths:

- a breath in as you go up to the light

- a breath out down to the Earth

- a breath in as you come back up

- a breath out as you expand your heart.

Here are examples of how some workshop attendees felt having done this TLC exercise:

- "I feel like smiling, like I could do anything in my business, that I could sell anything to anyone"

- "I feel more confident"

- "(If I was in a hiring interview, I would feel...) More patient, more compassionate, more hopeful maybe or open, possibility. Perceptive... More able to pick up stuff about the job candidates. More discerning."

If there's nothing else you practice from this book, learn how to do this.

Do it everyday. Preferably multiple times a day. In my experience, it makes my business run easier and useful coincidences just happen.

Other Ways to TLC

WWIT (What Would It Take) to connect to the light deeply today?

Some people like to walk in nature to TLC. Others swim. Or lie on the grass for a nap.

What can you do you in order to TLC regularly?

- I walk each morning to a large rock formation about five minutes away from where I live in Cusco. I sit on it in the dawn light and visualize connecting to the Earth. Then I stand up with my arms out and rotate slowing looking at the mountains and city saying Truth, Beauty, Love, Light.

- I do yoga each day for about 30 minutes, and meditate on my WWITs for the day.

- When I am in the shower, I imagine that each drop of water is a drop of love raining on me. Ditto for when it is raining outside.

- When I was in Barcelona, I would walk once a week to the beach about an hour after dawn for an early morning swim. It was very peaceful and restoring.

- There is something about salt water that draws out stuck emotions from my body. If I am not near the sea, I take salt baths (a cup of Epsom salts or regular salt + baking soda).

- I now have a habit where I check in during the day to make sure I am TLCed. And if not, I take a moment to reconnect to the light. If I notice I am feeling lower vibrations (sadness, anger, fear, etc.) I also do some clearing and reconnect to the light.

- I find five minutes of dancing to a happy song helps me TLC, too. I will do that in work breaks during my day. Helps get my energy back up, avoids back problems and it TLCs me!

Spirit Guide teacher Yamile Yemoonyah uses a rosary to come up with things to be grateful for every morning. She says, "It always raises my vibration and connects me to the light/universe/source."

Marketing consultant Nicole Seelinger told me that dancing helps her TLC:

"Dancing is awesome! Just letting the music flow through the body and moving it makes a huge impact for me (even if I'm simply sitting down and working). Rain indeed are drops of divine and I love appreciating it if I get caught in rain.

When I feel low emotions and vibrations, I tend to start feeling it physically in my body. Soon it becomes painful, and it used to be hard to make it pass (the physical pain would last longer than the emotion itself). So nowadays I start to imagine a pink light coming from the Universe entering my crown chakra and going to the place where I feel the emotion (or pain) and surround it with the pink light of divine love... It's been much easier to control it now when I do it soon enough not to let emotions turn into physical pain."

It is smart to notice pain in your emotional body before it spreads into the physical body. It is easier to move stuff there as it is less dense.

Measuring your Vibration Level

Now that you know several ways to TLC, let's look at a tool to measure your vibration level in detail. It will let you know when you are more likely to be successful in your business manifesting.

The Hawkins vibration level scale goes from 1 (very low) to 1000 (very high). From shame at 20, through fear (100), Desire (125), Love (500) and Enlightenment (700+). (From the book *"The Eye of the I"*).

To manifest, you want to be at 500+. It is hard to manifest anything when you are in a state of shame (20) because shame means "I am not enough." While desire is a major motivator for many people to change, the downside is that it can lead to addiction to things such things as sex, money, prestige, or power, so it does not make for effortless manifesting. Other issues prevent effortless manifesting at the other levels before 500. When you get to a vibration of 500 or above, you can easily manifest what you want in your life and business using your intuition.

Here are the common emotional levels on the Hawkins scale:

- Shame 20
- Guilt 30
- Apathy 50
- Grief 75
- Fear 100
- Desire 125
- Anger 150
- Pride 175
- Courage 200
- Neutrality 250
- Willingness 310
- Acceptance and Forgiveness 350
- Reason 400
- **Love 500**

- Joy 540

- Peace 600

- Gratitude 600-800

- Enlightenment 700-1000

To measure where you are on the scale, you can...

- Notice what emotion(s) you are feeling and the lowest one on the scale is your level.

- You can run your hand or eye down the list, and where it stops is your level.

- You can just ask your intuition what level you are currently at on the scale and see what number you get.

As we saw above, there are many techniques that will raise your vibration and help you TLC. From meditating to making gratitude lists to blessing yourself and others with light, the TLC tool lets you raise your vibration level fast.

When you have raised your vibration to 500+, then take those inspired actions out into the physical world. Make the phone call, send the email, or start the work that emerged from your intuition when you did your WWIT.

Doubt and Intuition

Many people confuse doubt and worry (which occur in the mind) with intuitive messages, which may come via body parts like the gut or in various other ways, such as hearing words, seeing images, noticing strange coincidences or seeing animals in an unusual place or manner.

I would recommend always investigating intuitive messages related to a decision, especially if they are strong or come to you in multiple ways (e.g., gut feeling, dream, several animal symbols on the same day). Do this by noting them in your intuition journal (discussed below) and asking your intuition what the deeper meaning of the message is. You can also ask other questions, such as "How will this decision improve my business in the longer term?" Or "How will my personal growth be affected by this?" After investigating, you will get more information on the decision, which either leads you towards a "Yes" or may lead you away to a "No."

As I explained above, I recommend replacing doubt and worry with TLC and WWIT. Instead of worrying about whether, say, a new hire will work out, connect to the light and ask yourself *"What Would It Take for this hire to work out?"*

If you are the kind of person that worries a lot, consider that **it may not be your worry**. It could be a family pattern of worry. Or you could be sensitive to other people's emotions and just be picking up their anxiety, or even your city's worry if things are in turmoil. If those factors could be at the root of your worries, clear your family's past and separate from other people's energy using the cord cutting tool below.

Trust your intuition. What would it take for you to trust your intuition twice as much as you do already? I know you already use your intuition in your work, through your sense of experience and gut feelings. You could use it more in your work, and the more you trust it, the more results you'll get.

To help in trusting your intuition more, you can keep an **intuition journal** — a record of the decisions you've made based on your intuition. It might be a paper journal or a spreadsheet. Record each decision that you make: What was the problem, and what was your decision? How did you make the decision? What intuitive messages did you hear? Come back to your journal periodically in future months to check which things worked, and which didn't. That way you can start to see which types of messages you should pay closest attention to.

An intuition journal provides the proof that you are capable of listening to your intuition and that it does work for you. This is especially true for those of us who get stuck in our heads worrying about whether we're going about things effectively.

Keeping a journal can also help to build your confidence in your ability. I encourage you to trust yourself. Many of us have self-doubt educated into us during school and through parenting, but the more you can delete that self-doubt and trust your own inner knowing, the more successful you can be and the more inspirational you can be to your clients.

Clearing Self-Sabotaging Business Beliefs

In my experience, most CEOs and entrepreneurs have self-sabotaging beliefs. Often these are subconscious, and you only know they are there because some part of your business is always a struggle, or because your revenue seems to be limited by an invisible ceiling.

Here is a case study with Gabby Wallace, CEO of Go Natural English. Her YouTube channel has millions of views and hundreds of thousands of subscribers. But she had some hidden beliefs that were holding her business back, and her energy was being drained by some of her clients:

> *"I have a lot of English learner followers who I don't personally know who comment on my personal profile (no longer so personal even with privacy settings) and comment*

on my new materials which are focused on YouTube marketing for entrepreneurs. It's harmless, but it is really seriously aggravating me. I guess there's some energy block or something. I'm thinking either I need to just let it go somehow and continue with my work, or maybe it's a message that I need to just focus on the English learners, since I've built up such an insanely loyal following. Thoughts?"

I said to her...

- How exactly do you aggravate yourself about this?

- When you think about it, what emotions do you notice? What do you notice in your body?

- What is the youngest age you felt the same way?

  - (Don't think about it; just say the first age that comes to mind, even if you have no memory of why. Ditto for the person it happened with. You don't have to know the "real" answer — a gut reaction is fine.)

- TLC (To the Light, Connect) yourself and send light to this younger version of you, clearing the pattern from your whole timeline. To do this, visualize light coming from above and below your younger self just like when you TLC yourself in the present time.

Gabby did this for about 10 minutes, then wrote back:

"Thanks Michael, great questions. I guess I choose feeling aggravated... I get angry because I feel like I'm not being listened to. I feel like despite whatever my message is, it's

falling on deaf ears, it doesn't seem to matter, and these fans are saying the same thing (I love you, teacher!). It's actually great and 99% positive attention, but my reaction is that my body gets tense, I feel like I'm suffocating, and like a ball of anger is growing inside my throat / chest (where we speak from!).

I felt this way the first time probably pretty young, but I'll say around 10 years old and I felt like my father wouldn't hear me. No matter what I wanted to express, it seemed to fall on deaf ears and I would get some weird comment of whatever he wanted to say totally unrelated to what I was trying to talk about. So I can see that I choose to get really bothered if I feel like someone is not listening and just seems to be having a conversation with themselves where I happen to be the recipient. Sending light to my younger self!"

After this first step, I also recommended that Gabby do some Cord Cutting with all her fans, and I'll explain this more in the next section. This intense attention is something many well-known or famous people have to deal with — you can try to think of someone in the public eye who deals with fan attention well, and model how they handle it.

About a week later, Gabby sent over an update.

"I just want to report back on how much improvement I've felt after working on unblocking some past stuff. I mentioned how angry & frustrated I would get when I receive off-topic or inappropriate comments on social media. Instead of making me feel angry, I was able to laugh this one off and

reply in what I think was a good way. I've been able to re-embrace my following with more love and dig deeper into that business. Thanks Michael and everyone for the support!"

Here is the **Facebook exchange Gabby is referring to:**

Mustapha L.: You are really cute. I'd like to guess you. I wanna marry you. Can you accept? I'm so serious and dreaming for Gorgeous like you. Cause only wow. They told me seen so good-looking. Please help me for coming there

Gabby Wallace: Thank you, Mustapha for your kind words. While that is a very nice offer, I would recommend that instead of marrying me, you take English lessons from me at Go Natural English.

After clearing this issue, Gabby also came up with an idea that adds 10% to her revenue for the year — an amazing ROI on 10 minutes of clearing work.

Office of the Mind

Your Office of the Mind is a place where you can access detailed intuitive information on your visions, goals and business.

TLC and close your eyes. Visualize an office with several meeting rooms and doors. Create an office where you have access to anything in the universe that you could use as a tool to create a better life, a better business, or to help other people in their lives or their businesses.

To give you some ideas of what you can create here, Chris Reynolds, CEO of Entrepreneur House, shared what he has in his Office of the Mind:

"I have two big, round tables where I sit down and talk to people about business or decisions in life that I need to make. I have a nice lounge area with sofas and some plants there, but we can sit and do some masterminding there, too. I also have a big screen in my Workshop where I see myself as I am today, then I see a picture of where I want to go or what I want to do. Then, I'll play that in a movie mode from where I am today to where I want to go, to see all the actions that I need to take to create whatever I want to create. I also have a room of infinity, I guess you could call it. I can go in there and just ask any questions, basically yes-or-no questions — "Should I do this, should I not" and get either green lights or red lights that show me if it's the right direction.

Other features in my Office of the Mind include a couple beds where, if there's friends or friends-of-friends that are sick or have physical ailments, they can come lay on the beds and then I'll have doctors from all around the world that can come in and work on them to help heal them. If I have any limiting beliefs, there's a big trashcan in the corner of it where I'll just dump any limiting beliefs and they boil away to nothing."

Here is how you might use your Office of the Mind:

Every work day after you meditate or just after waking, TLC (To the Light, Connect) then go to your Office of the Mind. Spend five minutes there solving problems in your business and your life, healing people, visualizing how you want your day to go. Then go about your day and see how well things are going.

If during your day a new problem comes up, you can TLC again and pop into your Office of the Mind to get help or answers.

Spiritual Advisory Board

The first room I suggest you create in your Office is your Spiritual Advisory Board meeting room. This is where you can bring in anyone to ask for advice in your business and life. Examples of who you can bring in:

- Successful business leaders (such Richard Branson or Tim Ferriss)
- People with special skills such as marketing, sales, legal, accounting, problem solving
- Ideal clients
- Ideal prospect avatars
- Past leaders (Henry Ford, John D Rockefeller)
- Future people or leaders (including your future self)
- Angels and guides (such as ArchAngel Ariel)
- Spiritual beings (such as Ganesha, Lakshmi, Odin, Jesus)
- Imaginary beings from books and movies (such as John Galt of "Atlas Shrugged" by Ayn Rand)

You can ask your board for advice on any business problems or goals you have. For example, if you are hiring, you could ask them which candidate will bring you the most profit and joy. You could ask WWIT to find an ideal candidate. When you are in your Spiritual Board Room, you can actually talk to them: "Hey, Richard, what do you think about this candidate? Why would she be good in this job? How much joy and profit will she bring me? WWIT to increase the joy and profit?" You will hear their reply in your mind.

Example: Suppose you and your team are creating an event for your business. Then you might ask your Board:

- What kind of event should we create?

- How many people do we want to attract to it?

- How is best to run it for more joy and profit?

- How do we want to feel and act during it?

- What type of experience should the attendees have?

- How much should we charge?

Whenever you have a major business decision to make, you can ask your Board for advice. Remember it is advice, not commands on what you must do. At the end of the day, you run your business, not your Board.

Record Board advice in your intuition journal as we discussed in Chapter 1. Write down your decisions and your Board's input. That way you can evaluate later how the decision worked out, and which Board members give useful advice (and which didn't). You can always remove Board members who are no longer useful and add new ones who are better suited to where your business is today. You can also invite people into a particular Board meeting but not have them join permanently.

You might be concerned that you have to ask permission in the physical world before bringing someone into your Spiritual Advisory

Board, but this is not the case. Firstly, you are, in effect, asking their Higher Self when you invite them into the room. And, secondly, you can welcome each person as they join your Board. You might offer them something in return for their being there. For example, you could send blessings to them, their family or friends, or help them spiritually with a challenge they have in their business or life. Or just "pay it forward" by helping someone not on your Board.

You are not limited to having other entrepreneurs for your Board. Chris Reynolds told me that he sometimes invites Gandhi, Jesus and Mother Teresa. You can invite dead people as well as the living.

You can invite anybody. You just enter your Boardroom of the Mind and visualize whoever you want to get advice from.

They don't even have to be real people. You could invite some of the X-Men if their super powers would be useful. Or maybe Quark, the Ferengi businessman from Star Trek Deep Space Nine, if you thought he might have some good ideas on a particular business deal.

Even spiritual beings such as angels and gods can be helpful. For example, Ganesha, the Hindu god with an elephant head, and his friend the rat, are good at removing obstacles. Or Lakshmi, the Hindu goddess of wealth, fortune and prosperity might help bring more abundance to your business if you asked her for advice.

Who Do You Invite In?

You might set some criteria for who you invite into your Board. For example, I like to have beings of high vibration (500 = love or higher on the Hawkins scale from Chapter 1) and who are beneficial for me.

If you want to get advice from someone who is skilled in one area but you don't like in other areas of their life, then you can filter them to just bring the area you want into your Board.

For example, you might bring in the deal-making skills of Donald Trump into your board, but leave out his other characteristics, or invite in his younger self if you prefer that to his current-day self.

Maybe you like how Genghis Khan expanded his empire so fast, but are not so keen on how his army killed so many people. You just bring in his genius of organization, but you don't bring in the violence. You're in control of your Office of your Mind. Genghis can really get things moving — he is worth chatting to. Just be cautious if he recommends expanding your business into Mongolia!

Your Other Selves

You can also invite past and future versions of yourself. Your future self may have a better perspective on your problems, or may know how you solved them in the past, or could share issues to avoid where there was a mistake made on your timeline.

Chris Reynolds invites his ninety-five-year-old future self to his board. He says of him:

> "In times where I experience a lot of distress, I'll sit and talk to him and he's just like, 'Calm down, kid. Everything's going to be okay. You're going to have a great life. Everything's turning out really well.' He's cool."

I recommend inviting younger versions of yourself to your Office of the Mind. Many of our beliefs and patterns are formed between conception and the age of seven. Our subconscious mind is controlled by these beliefs. Often as an adult, we don't understand why we still do the things we do, especially self-sabotaging behavior. This is often because most of our actions are controlled by our subconscious mind.

You can talk to your younger self and ask questions. "Why am I doing this?" Then your younger self might say, "Oh, that's because of this event that happened when you were 3 years old and we created this belief in your subconscious mind which you are now repeating over and over and over again. By the way, you copied this belief from your father, which he got from his parents, and so on."

At that point, you might invite your father and all his ancestors with this belief into your Office of the Mind so that you can clear yourself and all of them at the same time. One way to clear the belief is to TLC (To the Light, Connect) the belief. Visualize the belief as a web of light in front of you and see lots of light coming into it from above and below until it shifts and dissolves from your reality.

Similarly, you can invite in past life versions of yourself for advice, information and clearing, and the same goes for future versions of yourself.

Room of Infinity: Green Light/Red Light

Another useful room to add to your Office of the Mind is your Room of Infinity. It is a door in your Office that leads to an infinite room of nothing — the void. You can go in and ask Yes/No questions. For a yes answer, you will see a green light and for a no, you will see a red light.

You might think of this room as a direct connection to Source/the Universe/God. Of course, this is your Office and you have free will. Even if you get a red light, you can still decide to go ahead with that decision. For example, you might have asked your Room of Infinity, "Will I be happy hiring this person?" and got a red light/no. Or perhaps you ask "Should I continue to employ this person?" and got a red light, but you still kept them in their job. Then later you might notice that things didn't work out so well or that there were negative consequences.

Again, I recommend you record your decisions in your Intuition Journal together with the questions you asked your Room of Infinity and what response it gave.

Chris Reynolds had the following experience with his Room of Infinity:

> *"I asked it about Facebook ads. I definitely got a green light for doing them. It ended up being a good lesson in my life, but I didn't end up making money from them"*

This is an important point — the quality of the question determines the quality of the answer. "Should I do Facebook ads" is a simple-level question. "Will Facebook ads be profitable for me in the next year?" would be a better question. In the first case, it might be that you should do them to have the experience of creating something new, even if it loses money. In the second case, if you get the green light, you will make money with them.

Different answers come from your intuition depending on what questions you ask, so make sure you are being specific and clear.

Relationship Table

You can add a Relationship Table to your Office of the Mind. This is a place where you invite spiritual advisors who can coach you on improving your relationships, whether they are relationships with employees, clients, vendors, friends, family or romantic relationships. You could ask whether this person is a good fit for your business or personal life, and whether to see them more or less. WWIT (What Would It Take) to attract new ideal people into each role?

For example, if you have a client who is getting a little challenging to work with, you could ask your relationship coaches, "WWIT to improve our relationship? Should I continue with them or not?" This can save you a lot of headaches, time and money over the years.

Cord Cutting

Cords drain your energy and can hold you back in your business. A negative energy cord attaches you to another person or past trauma, and cutting them frees up more of your precious energy for your goals.

A business friend of mine wrote me their experience on cord cutting:

> *"Today I was on a mastermind call where I had a hot seat. I went in feeling good and very optimistic about my direction. Then for several hours afterwards, I felt tired, down, grouchy and uncertain. These were the exact emotions that the guy who was dominating the conversation had — he isn't sleeping because he is doing a crazy launch. I realized that those feelings were not mine. They even felt foreign. Odd!*
>
> *It was effective enough for me to just remember you mentioning the cord cutting, becoming aware of what had happened and intuitively clearing it — (the negative emotion) was gone immediately.*
>
> *I totally see how cords others put out have been energy sucks. And I have been conscious about being with people close to me without making meaning out of what they are saying and allowing their energy to pull me down. That way, I can*

support them through a rough day and not get myself tangled in it."

To cut a cord, you imagine an actual rope connecting you with someone or something else. Then imagine a sword or scissors cutting the cord. As with all business magic, it relies on both the decision you make and the energetic power you put behind it. In case you are freaking out by my use of the term "business magic," my definition of that is *anything we do energetically that affects the physical world of our business.*

Examples of business magic include:

- Shifting a negative team spirit to a positive one

- Aligning staff to your vision for the business

- Setting clear intention on what kind of staff and clients you want in your business.

- Attracting ideal clients to your business

- Turning around an upset client energetically before you call them

CEO Josh Plotkin says on this topic:

"Michael likes to use the word magic to describe what he does, and the results he gets often seem like magic. Some of his techniques may seem kind of out there, but at the end of the day, they deliver greater emotional stability and mental clarity. If you're facing a roadblock in your life or business that you can't seem to overcome, talk to Michael and let him work his magic on you."

I recommend TLC before cord cutting to give you more power. A prayer can also provide both decision and power because when you pray, you may connect to your higher self, angel, guide or god.

The most common angel asked to help in cord cutting is Archangel Michael (AAM) who is a warrior of light and carries a powerful sword to help with the cutting.

To cut a lot of cords, first ask your intuition how many cords you have in total with a particular person. Then you can either cut them one at a time or, once you are practiced in cord cutting, cut a bunch of them at once. There may be a few stubborn ones to deal with individually. As well as asking how many cords you have with one person, you can ask how many you have in total, with anyone. This helps you keep track of how you are doing with your cord cutting and makes you more aware of cords you might have missed.

As well as cutting the cord, it is important to heal the part of your body where it was connected, so that the pattern that attracted or allowed the cord is no longer active. Ask your intuition to show you where the cord was attached and how you allowed it to attach. You can also ask questions to the cord to find out details on the pattern. What was the age you first had a cord attach to you, who it was with, what it was about? That can help clear your cords faster because the more consciousness you have about an issue, the easier it is to clear.

For example, I might have a cord from a client in my right abdomen and the pattern might be that I don't feel worthy, so I don't speak up about excessive demands from them.

To heal, imagine a powerful waterfall of light on the part of the body you felt the cord was attached to until the area feels better. You can imagine the same waterfall of light clearing the pattern that allowed this cord to connect in the first place.

I always recommend this cleansing step after cord cutting, because if you don't, it is common for the person to try to reattach the cord. You may notice this — often they will phone, text or email you soon after cutting. Even if you have not seen them in years, they feel the energetic shift and want to try to reconnect the cord to you. By clearing your body and the pattern, they can't reattach and your energy remains strong.

Note that cords can be high vibration (love energy) or low vibration. You only need to cut the low vibration ones. Don't worry about "accidentally" cutting the high vibration cords you want to keep, as you can set your intent when cutting that only low vibration ones will be cut.

It is good to cut cords with everyone you meet. I do it after every...

- Client session
- Group meetings (lots of cutting during conferences!)
- After a hug or handshake
- Especially with friends and family (because we are more likely to form cords with people we are emotionally close to)

Business Energy Spring Cleaning

It's also a good idea to cut cords with past relationships and meetings, especially repeated ones. I made a list to cord cut of past...

- employees
- vendors
- clients
- romantic relationships

You can also have cords from past-life relationships with the same person. These can be stronger cords (see below for tips on cutting these) and can be a particularly strong energy drain for you and your business.

People who are energy vampires for you are especially good at making cords with you, because they are a fit for your attraction pattern. A common pattern is victim/perpetrator. The perpetrator cords to the victim and sucks energy from them. Another common pattern is helper/taker. Often there are multiple cords connecting you to a person. They may even go in a circle where you have cords back to the other person creating an energy circuit. While that sounds like it might be energy neutral, in reality it drains both people.

You can cut cords for...

- someone else

- pets

- your bank account

- your business

- your home

As with all psychic work, drink lots of water, electrolytes, rest and make sure to connect to the light (TLC) before and after cord cutting.

Q: So, if you only have to cut cords with lower vibrations, why do it after every hug, session or group interaction? What if they were high vibration?

A: Because if I have the rule or habit to cut cords after every hug, session or group interaction, I save time and mental energy on asking are there any negative cords left from it. When I cut cords, I set the intention that only lower vibration cords are cut, any love or high vibration ones remain. So there is no risk of losing love from this method and it keeps my energy space clean.

It is similar to the reason I have a habit of wiping my shoes on the doormat every single time I enter my home. I could check if I have dirt on my shoes every time I come in, which takes extra thought power and time, or just use the habit and move on. There is no downside and it keeps my space clean.

Q: How will I know if I'm cutting cords properly?

A: You will feel a shift in your body and energy. Often the other people will react, too — you might get an unexpected email or call. You will feel better - lighter and with a higher vibration on the Hawkins scale. You might have a brief detox reaction first - that would feel like having a cold or nausea for 30 minutes.

Is This Your Energy?

A good way to test if cords are involved if you are feeling low energy or a negative emotion is to ask your intuition:

- Is this energy mine?

If you are an empathic person, as many leaders are, you may find about 50% of what you feel is not even your stuff!

If it is yours, then use the clearing tools above to release it. If it is not yours, then either cut the cord from it or ask *"WWIT to separate from this energy?"* Or you can simply declare *"What is mine is mine and I release all else."*

What Health Routines Keep You Grounded and in Touch With Your Intuition?

In this area, everyone is different. I would ask your own intuition, *"What would it take for me to be more in contact with my own intuition?"* See what comes to you.

Personally I find walking everyday and getting out in nature makes all the difference. If I'm feeling overwhelmed from social situations, just getting away from other people can help reset my intuition.

If there are people who are energy vampires in my life or in my business, I make sure to remove them. Spring cleaning your Facebook friends would be a small example of that. If there are people who drain your energy when you read their stuff, just remove them. They won't know if you remove them, but you will know because you will feel better. If Facebook drains your energy, then remove Facebook from your phone.

I also do yoga and I meditate. I listen to my body. My body will often tell me if there's something I need to be doing differently. I try not to have rigid rules, but to go with the flow, listen to what my body or spirit is telling me in the moment. What I may need today may be different from what I needed yesterday.

Homeplay

- Play with using WWIT (What Would It Take) today when you have a worry or problem

- Try different ways of TLC (To the Light, Connect) and notice which works best for you.

- Experiment with cord cutting and notice what changes occur in your business

- Create your own Office of the Mind and play with it each day for a few minutes

- Invite useful and fun people to your Spiritual Advisory Board and ask them for advice on current challenges in your business.

- Journal about your decisions and the advice you got from your Board in your Intuition Journal

- Ask yourself: WWIT for you to be more in touch with your intuition today?

Bonus Materials

The bonus materials from this chapter are at
www.intuitiveleadershipmastery.com/bonus/

- How to TLC (To the Light, Connect) (video)

- Interview about Office of the Mind with Chris Reynolds (audio)

CHAPTER 2

10x Your Business Intuition

"Cease trying to work everything out with your minds. It will get you nowhere. Live by intuition and inspiration and let your whole life be Revelation." - *Eileen Caddy co-founder of Findhorn Foundation Community*

A common belief is that we are stuck with the amount of intuition skill that we were born with. That is not true on two levels. First, you can dramatically increase your intuition levels, even 10x the amount you had to begin with. Secondly, babies and small children usually have amazing levels of intuition. Unfortunately, it gets covered up by taking on beliefs from our parents, school, work, religion, military and more institutions in our society.

In this chapter, we look at different ways you can increase your business intuition so that you can increase your profits and joy faster, and reduce your stress, too.

Is It Really My Intuition?

It is common for leaders new to using intuition in their business to doubt the intuitive information they receive. How can you distinguish between business intuition and a personal bias *disguised* as intuition?

Firstly, TLC (To the Light, Connect) before asking your intuition questions, because then the messages you get will be from your higher truth and not your ego field.

Secondly, you can look for intuitive answers in different ways to confirm or deny the intuitive answer that you first got. The more different ways you receive the same message, the more likely it is that it's coming from your intuition and not your ego. For example, you might look at your dreams for messages, or see what your different body parts have to say, or do muscle testing or ask an intuitive friend what she gets in answer to your question.

Is Intuition Always Right?

Is intuition always right, or are there cases that your intuition can fail you? It is easy to let ego/personal bias creep into what we might wish is our intuition.

The quality of the questions you ask your intuition affects the quality of the answers you will get back. For example, moving down this list of questions gives an increasing quality of answers:

- Is it good to hire candidate A?

- Will candidate A bring me joy and profits?

- Will candidate A bring me joy and profits this year?

- What do the joy and profit graphs of candidate A look like?

In particular, a Yes from your intuition to the first question does not guarantee a Yes to the second question. (The hire might be good for you because they create a crisis in your business, making you aware of a deep-seated spiritual block that you then get the opportunity to heal.)

If you TLC (To the Light, Connect) before you ask questions of your intuition, then you are connecting to universal truth and that helps you get better answers.

Personally, I find that messages from my gut or hips are clearer and more likely to be true than messages from my head or heart. The head is often full of other people's ideas and my own beliefs, and my heart is full of my and other people's emotions. This is why you are more likely to hear top business leaders say they go with their gut rather than their heart.

Clearing Common Blocks to Intuition

The most common block to intuition is to think that you don't have it or that it does not exist for you. Really, everyone has intuition, but many people have learned to tune it out.

Usually our intuition is a quiet voice, and if you have a lot of distractions in your mind and body, you won't hear it. It is like your intuition is a passenger in your car talking to you in a soft voice, but you have the car radio turned up to max volume so as not to hear them.

Similarly, if you avoid quiet time by always watching/listening to TV, radio, internet, or cell phone checking, then it will be harder to hear your intuition.

Other addictions such as alcohol, drugs, smoking, food, shopping and sex are often used to avoid being quiet. It is as though the ego is afraid to be quiet because then it might hear some messages from the intuition that it is afraid of, or hear the negative monkey mind messages that it does not like.

This is why meditation, going to a quiet space and yoga all help with hearing your intuition better. These practices help to quiet the mind.

Part of the work of getting quiet is realising that you are not your mind. You are a spiritual being who has a mind. Not all the thoughts that come through your mind are worth listening to, especially if they come from one of the thousands of advertisements that the typical adult sees and hears each day. Ads are distracting, and feed a sense of lack and dissatisfaction that blurs our ability to see what is really important to us.

If you are challenged by the idea of quiet time, then a good way to start is to join a class or group of people who are committed to practicing the form of quiet time you are attracted to. For example, you could join a yoga class or group meditation or attend a silent retreat. You might have a digital detox day each week where you don't watch any TV, listen to any radio, or see movies or internet for the day. Instead, go out in nature to walk or rest or play.

Another common block to receiving intuitive messages is the belief that you must get your intuition in a certain way. For example, that you must *hear* the voice of your intuition. There are many ways you can receive intuition, far beyond just hearing things. Here are some common ways to receive intuitive messages:

- Hearing voices in your head

- Seeing images with eyes closed or open

- Dreams

- Just knowing the answer

- Feelings in your body

- Smelling

- Animal signs

- Coincidences

Be open to different ways you may get information. There is no one right way.

How Do I Know If It's Fear, Ego or Intuition?

To tell if it is your intuition or fear talking, check in with your body — how do you feel with this information? If you feel open or expansive, or experience a sense of peace or love, or it "rings true," then it is usually intuition. If you contract, or feel small, anxious or fearful, then it is usually fear or your ego talking.

When you connect with your intuition, you can connect to different levels of truth. You really want to connect with the universal truth, but if your energy is small or fearful, it can stop you from fully connecting with the light, so you end up connecting more with your ego. That's where a lot of people run into issues and have to ask, *"Is this really my intuition, or is this my ego talking, or is it someone else talking?"*

Many CEOs and entrepreneurs are very intuitive and very sensitive to other people's energy. That's why we're often able to work well with people. On the other hand, if we're around people too much, we pick up what *they* want instead of what we want, which is another reason why it is good to TLC every day. Learn to separate from other people's energy using cord cutting (see chapter 1), or regularly go outside into nature and get away from other people to meditate and connect with your intuition.

WWIT to trust your intuition more?

What Would It Take to trust yourself and your intuition more?

An intuition journal where you record your decisions and the intuitive information you receive about them can help. You can review past decisions and see how following or not following your intuition worked out.

This is good if you are new to using your intuition because you can continue to make decisions using your traditional logical methods, then check in with what your intuition has to say afterwards. That reduces the risk of changing suddenly to a new method of using your intuition.

It also encourages you to practice your intuition daily. Intuition is like a muscle — if you don't work out regularly, it can shrink.

On the other hand, if you listen and act on your intuition, it will grow. It is like taking inspired actions from your intuition makes you hear it better in the future.

You can make it grow faster by doing a daily gratitude practice where you speak or write down all the intuitive information that you are grateful for having received today.

Fear of Using Intuition

Many people fear to use their intuition or to discuss openly that they use it. Intuition is traditionally frowned upon in Western social institutions: school, work, religion, government.

If you are a student in school and you get the right answer from your intuition rather than your rational mind, you may be punished for "cheating." Similarly, many businesses expect you to back up decisions with a logical argument. Some religions teach that intuition comes from the devil and should be ignored.

Often parents tell children who have "imaginary friends" or who hear voices to stop listening to these messages because "grown-ups don't do these things" or because of a fear of looking silly in front of others. They may be just repeating to their children what their parents told them.

Changing Beliefs Tool: *The Work* by Byron Katie

If you fear using your intuition, then becoming conscious of the exact beliefs you have about it can help. Write them down and question if each belief is true using the following questions:

- Is it true? (Yes or no. If no, move to 3.)

- Can you absolutely know that it's true? (Yes or no.)

- How do you react, what happens, when you believe that thought?

- Who would you be without the thought?

These questions are part of *The Work* by Byron Katie. It is an easy way for clearing non-useful beliefs. You can get a free guide to *The Work* and a guide to how to use them at her website http://thework.com/

You can also use the Youngest Age Pattern Recycling tool from Chapter 6. In summary, you think about the belief. Notice how you feel in your emotions and body when you think about it. Then ask yourself what is the youngest age you felt the same way? With who? Then TLC (To the Light, Connect) that younger version of you — see light coming into them from above and below, clearing the belief you no longer need.

- WWIT to swap in a new lens of playful experimentation with new ways?

- WWIT to let your squirrel retire? Thank it for protecting you as best as it could and wave goodbye to it.

It may be that you are carrying negative energy about intuition from other people around you, ancestors or past lives. You can cord-cut from each of these people, healing them and you by TLC-ing yourself and them.

Many CEOs are empathic to other people's energy, so learning how to separate your energy from others can help you hear your intuition more clearly.

Many intuitive people had a past life or ancestors where they were punished, tortured or killed for using their intuitive skills. The Spanish Inquisition and witch hunts in other countries attacked millions of intuitive practitioners, so if you are descended from those people, you may have some ancestral fears of using your skills in this lifetime, to discuss them openly or to profit from them.

Perhaps you have had experiences either in the past in this lifetime or you've had past lifetimes where using your intuition openly in business was a route to fear, pain or even death. That would tend to make you avoid what you need to do to grow your business using your intuition.

You are hiding your true powers, protecting yourself in your past lives where you got punished in various violent ways for this kind of thing.

Unfortunately, this might mean you act completely counterproductively to what you say you want to achieve in your business. You're sabotaging yourself by avoiding your intuition.

You can clear these issues by TLCing yourself, your past selves and ancestors and seeing them being healed. The energy rewrite process (see the chapter on advanced tools) can help, too.

- WWIT for you to feel your intuition fully?

- WWIT for it to be safe, right and good for you to feel your intuition fully?

- What message are you afraid of hearing?

We've all seen that in our businesses. We take two steps forward and one step back because there's part of us, either from our own childhood or from a past life, that is afraid. There's something dangerous about having this business and getting it to grow. Things from past lives can get lodged in the consciousness.

Even if you don't have anything like that, it's not like being an intuitive person is encouraged in school. It's more likely to get you labelled as a freak. I don't remember the career counselor saying, "You should hone your sense of intuition so you can go and create a company that gives you a vibrant life!" It was more like... "Get a steady job in a corporate firm, work for 40 years and retire with a nice watch."

When you use your intuition, it's the truth. And this immediate access to the truth can be scary to you and others. If you're really listening to your intuition, then nothing can stop you. You might not want to face that powerful side of you. So instead you hit blocks and fears, and this chapter and the Intuition Toolbox chapter are designed to help you overcome those issues.

Dealing With Doubt

The question you ask your intuition determines the quality of the information you're going to get back from it.

For example...

- Will this customer be good for me?

- Will this customer bring me joy and profits?

A "yes" answer to the first question does not imply the second question is a "yes," also. Perhaps the customer will cause a crisis in your business which will make you aware of an old pattern that you can now heal. Is that good? Yes, from your higher-self's point of view, but it may not be what you were looking for in a "good" client.

But how do you know that your subconscious isn't interfering with the answer?

Tell it not to. Ask for the truth. Connect to the light, ask for the truth. Doubt is the opposite of certainty, so bring in the energy of certainty.

Doubt is not always bad, though. Doubt can be a signal of intuition. For example, if you have done a logical analysis of a job candidate, and it seems good "on paper," but you have an intuitive doubt, then the answer on whether you should hire that person is a "no."

If you don't feel confident about working with someone, I would definitely not hire them or have them as a client. Doubt is an evolutionary tool, designed to save us from missteps. It gets in the way a lot, but it serves as a very effective warning system when something just isn't quite right.

In this case, the doubt is a message from your intuition. An uneasy feeling in your stomach is a veto on hiring. If you want to go further into it, you could ask "Where is this uneasy feeling coming from? Is it something about me? Or is it something about them?"

Or if you really want to hire this person, you could work on shifting the energy of unease. You could do healing or magic to shift the situation.

Same thing with profit graph for a candidate. If you feel the profit graph is flat, you can ask "WWIT to get it to go up?" And then you see if you get inspirations to improve the situation or you can use any of the other tools in this book to shift your reality. You can use intuition to get your information, but you can also then manipulate reality to get what you want.

Action Helps Intuition

The more I act on my intuition, the stronger it gets and the easier it becomes to hear it.

The universe responds best to action. WWITs, prayer and meditation are all good. When you take an action towards what you want, you are far more likely to see results — even if they come from unexpected quarters. Start moving and the universe starts moving, too.

If you're stuck on what your next action should be, do a WWIT to work it out. There is no excuse for not having a next step to move onto with this tool, so keep taking consistent action until you reach your goal.

Focusing On Happy Intuition

A daily practice where you answer the following questions can help build your intuition.

1) Today I am grateful for my intuition because ___

2) Today I helped someone with my intuition by ___

3) Something about my intuition that made me happy today was ___

4) Today I learned ___ about my intuition.

5) Tomorrow I will ___ (using my intuition)

Concerns About Reading the Future

Some of the intuition tools we cover in this book, such as the joy graph in Chapter 5 (sales), are about predicting the future. You might feel concerned about that.

Intuition can be used for prediction. It can give you more information about the future (and the present and the past). You're getting more information about yourself and other dimensions.

It is a way of reaching through what is unknown to our conscious, rational mind. If you have fears or a sense of discomfort about predicting what's going to happen in the future, I have a small exercise that will help you through it.

When a phone rings, I know who's ringing more than 80% of the time (with no caller ID). When an instant message comes in, I know who it is before I even go into the program to find who it is.

If you want to improve that skill, every time your phone rings or an IM comes in, ask yourself who it is before you look at the caller ID. Then see if you are right. The more you practice using your intuition, the better it gets.

Having done this exercise, you will learn to feel okay about predicting a few seconds in the future. If you're still not okay taking it a year into the future, then it's just a scale issue. WWIT to be okay about reading a year into the future?

The real answer is that there is no such thing as time or space.

You know that you can do affirmations to create the future you want. That's a way of manipulating the future. We're doing WWIT and changing the future to unfold as you want it to. So you can already read the future. You can change it. There is no time. It's all one time. We're just pretending that we have one current time. That's why you can access the future with your intuition.

The key point here is that:

We are not human beings having a spiritual experience, running a business stuck in the current time. We are spiritual beings having a human experience, running a business on this planet in this section of time.

And in other words, we are all gods with a body and a business, able to do anything we want to on this planet.

Intuition is just another tool that you can use in your business. Just like your rational mind is a tool or a spreadsheet is a tool. The only questions then are:

- Does this tool work for me?

- Is this the right tool for the issue at hand?

By keeping a journal of decisions you've made using rational thought, intuition or a combination, you can see what your intuition is truly capable of. For example, you record in your decision journal that you decided to hire someone for X, Y and Z reasons (including your rational reasoning and any intuitive messages you received). Then six months later you come back and check out: Was my gut feeling on this good? Or was it bad? Was I thinking of hiring someone, but didn't and then heard from their next placement that they turned into a disaster zone? This is how you can increase your confidence in using your intuition.

Getting Information and Risk

If you're in business, is it useful to be able to get information when you haven't studied something inside and out, having analyzed every logical detail? Yes.

Is it useful to be able to hire someone quickly who's the right fit for your company without going through a lot of having to interview a hundred different people? Yes.

Using the tools from Chapter 4 on Hiring, you can just feel which person is the right fit. Interview that person first. Then if your intuition wasn't firing so well right then, you pick the next one when you get your next intuitive message. You don't have to go through your whole list one at a time in a logical way.

An important question to ask yourself is this: What risks are you willing to take solely on the basis of intuition?

As long as I connect to the light and I'm feeling good, I'm at a point that I will trust my intuition on just about any decision. If I'm feeling anxious and distracted and small, then I know there's far more risk and that I need to wait until I'm more connected to the universe. But if i'm feeling expansive, then I go with it. That is why using the TLC tool is so important, because it helps you feel expansive and connected and clear.

If you are only using your intuition as a check on things after you have done other types of analyses, then consider flipping that. Do the intuition work first, and then once you've picked something, you could do a little logical check to see if the intuition made any logical sense. That would be faster and help you to build your intuition confidence.

Hearing Messages and Ringing In The Ears

CEO Tal Gur told me a story recently where he was ignoring his intuition, and then experienced ringing in his ears:

> *"There was a point like two years ago where my ex-partner and I were thinking of moving to the U.S. She wanted us to move to the U.S. I wasn't sure about that, and the first time we talked about it, I remember I wanted to vomit. And I wasn't sure where it was coming from, because I hadn't eaten anything bad.*
>
> *At the same time, I started to develop tinnitus (ringing in the ears).*

I went to doctors, specialists, and they all told me, 'It's incurable, you're probably going to have it for the rest of your life.' But the minute that I left the U.S., it changed. I got my hearing back."

Often ringing in the ears is spiritual messaging from angels or guides. They're communicating that you're not hearing an important message, and it comes in as ringing. If I say to my guides "I'd like to hear what you're saying, but all I'm hearing is ringing — can you show me the message another way?" Then the ringing stops and I'll get the message. Either I'll hear it, or I'll get some sign or another. That works for me.

I'm guessing that Tal's angels and guides were probably trying to send him a message, but he was not listening and didn't ask them to tell him a different way. But as soon as he didn't need the message anymore, after he had left the country, it went away.

The key here is to always listen to your body, even if it is in pain or has an illness. In many ways, your body is smarter than your mind.

Guided Universe, Inner GPS, Beliefs and Truth

What is the guided universe? It is the belief that the universe is not random and that you can trust it.

All the synchronicities that can happen can be explained away as coincidence. But when a lot of synchronicities happen, it just doesn't make sense to label them as coincidences. When you have a lot of synchronicities in your life, it's not random. The universe is guiding and all you have to do is listen.

In writing this book, I was listening to the universe. It didn't come from a logical place. I never saw myself as an author, and I never thought I would publish anything about intuition — it was just something I enjoyed sharing with others. But now it feels like something that is much bigger than me. It's something I had to do, but even knowing that, I had resistance to creating it. I procrastinated on writing, editing and marketing it, but fortunately I had the tools in the book to clear that, and magical friends to help me, too.

When you get a message from the universe, it tends to repeat itself. That's often a clue that it is a message from the intuition — it comes in several different ways. I also find that with messages from my body. If I have a pain or disease in a part of my body, that's usually a message. If I ignore it, it gets worse until I face it, or it will pop up somewhere else. When I hear it, that part of the body gets better.

I really recommend that you take note of these messages. Even if you are suspicious about the whole intuition thing and you are still questioning it, delve into knowing yourself better. Once you know yourself, really know yourself, you'll understand why you're here. Then the whole idea of a guided universe makes sense.

Learning to trust and use your intuition more involves change.

(And if you find this change challenging, then think about what the worst thing that could happen would be. A lot of times we imagine the worst, but even the worst is not really so bad. You can always go back to your old life. Treat changes as experiments. This is your intuition experiment.)

Some people have difficulty with change because they have beliefs that get in their way. We all have beliefs, it's just our operating system. Beliefs affect our emotions and become the filter through which we see our reality.

But the most important belief is what you *believe* about your beliefs. Are they fixed forever, or can you become conscious of them and change them?

At a deep level, I believe that beliefs are not true. They are useful or not useful in a certain situation, they can be changed, and I find that very empowering.

Every belief serves you to some extent. Maybe you have a belief about yourself that keeps you small and safe from being big out in the world. The belief is trying to protect you, but it's also stifling you and your business.

Once you realize these things, you have more choice — the choice to choose a different belief.

But again, the most important belief is the belief about beliefs. If you don't believe that you can change beliefs in a split second, that will be your reality. It is harder to change your beliefs if you don't think it can be done.

The key questions for changing beliefs are from *The Work* by Byron Katie:

1. Is it true? (Yes or no. If no, move to 3.)
2. Can you absolutely know that it's true? (Yes or no.)
3. How do you react, what happens, when you believe that thought?
4. Who would you be without the thought?

Choose beliefs that empower you. Put them on like fresh new clothes and trade them in when they don't serve you anymore. This is your life, your business, and every belief you have affects how they unfold. Don't get stuck in fixed beliefs that limit you, that disconnect you from love and intuition.

Living in Fear or Love

Many people live in a lot of fear in traditional jobs, doing things that they don't like doing. What if instead you could do whatever your intuition led you to, and could be without that fear?

WWIT to trust your intuition completely?

Once you can trust your intuition like this, you will find that it greatly reduces the amount of fear that you experience.

At a deep level, there's nothing to fear really when you think about it.

One of the motivations I have for writing this book is that things are changing in the world more and more rapidly. Technology is changing, society is changing, the planet is changing. It's hard to run a business with all of the change and all of the decisions that have to be made, if we have to make all of the decisions rationally. It's much quicker to use intuition to read what is going on and use business magic to make the decisions turn out correctly for you.

If all of the businesses on the planet would run using intuition as well as their rational mind, just think how much more efficient the world's businesses would be, how much happier all of the people working in them and customers of them would be. And I don't think we would have all of these crazy things some businesses get up to that are very destructive now, just because that wouldn't make sense to intuition to do that.

Intuition As a Tool

Intuition is a tool and the rational mind is a tool. Tools are designed to get you what you want in life. For me, just using the rational mind doesn't give me everything I want in life.

Both tools serve us on the same level. You can choose at every single moment whether to use your logical mind or to use your intuition. You can talk with them to get both perspectives — you are not your thoughts, or your feelings. Those parts of yourself are tools that you can use as an observer of your life. You can always choose what tools to use, choosing the right tool based on the situation you are currently facing.

If Your Intuition Is Blocked by Others' Opinions:

Intuition is often a quiet inner voice, so helps me to get to a quiet space, meditate, take a walk in nature, sleep, before I listen to it.

It helps to cord cut from strong, opinionated people before you access intuition. I would recommend you cord cut from everyone, just to be sure you are not being influenced by them.

Connecting to the light with TLC and expanding your heart helps connect to more universal truth rather than "local truth." When your energy is contracted (e.g., in space of ego or fear) you tend to access local truth.

Silence and Vipassana

Silence helps you hear your intuition. One way to strengthen your "silence muscle" is to do a silent retreat. The most well-known one is called Vipassana. Vipassana is a multi-day silent retreat. You sit in one place, usually for 12 hours a day for 10 days.

You get the opportunity to observe all of the crazy thoughts you have and all of the wacky emotions. You think about your thoughts. You observe your thoughts. It can get weird.

But then you learn to not be so attached to your thoughts and emotions. You realize that they come and go, and that they are separate from *you*.

Perhaps 10 days of silence sounds extreme.

For many people, even 10 minutes of silence would be extreme. We listen to music, we have our phones, social media, TV. Many people don't even know where they would find 10 minutes of complete peace and quiet each day, but that would be a good place to start. Find a few minutes of peace in your life, focus on your breath and let your intuition start to rise to the top of your mind.

> *"You get your intuition back when you make space for it, when you stop the chattering of the rational mind. The rational mind doesn't nourish you. You assume that it gives you the truth, because the rational mind is the golden calf that this culture worships, but this is not true. Rationality squeezes out much that is rich and juicy and fascinating."* - Anne Lamott, writer and activist.

Minute Breath

Here is a way to start with silence so you can hear your intuition better. It is a simple yoga technique called minute-breath, where you inhale for 20 seconds, hold your breath for 20 seconds, and then exhale for 20 seconds.

If you can't get to a whole minute, you just start off 5 seconds in, 5 seconds hold, 5 seconds out, or whatever number you're comfortable with. Just doing a short period of minute-breath will totally change how you feel. It will give you more peace, and no one needs to know you're doing it. You can be in a business meeting that's gotten a bit crazy, you can be in an intense discussion in a relationship you're in, you can be in a supermarket line, you can be at a red light in your car. You can choose consciously to change your breath.

And the powerful thing is that when you shift your breath and energy, it shifts all the people around you. Things become calm. You return to peace. Try it next time you are with others who are tense, anxious or angry.

We talked about this consciously, but it also happens unconsciously. If you're in an argument with your romantic partner, and you start to change your breath, they will change their breath without even knowing it.

The same thing happens if you're in a sales meeting or some other business meeting. If you change your breath, other people will change or shift how they feel. It's a powerful tool for effecting change.

Everyone is able to control their breathing.

It's also detoxifying, it's great for metabolism. If we realized how beneficial it is, we probably would be far more conscious of the way we're breathing. Most people don't breathe correctly. It sounds crazy, because it's something we don't even think about doing, but most people breathe very shallowly. And many people breathe in reverse.

If you have taken a yoga class, then you probably know that when you breathe in, ideally your stomach and abdomen comes out as you breathe in, expanding the lungs, and as you breathe out, you contract your stomach. More than half the people in the United States breathe backwards. When they're breathing in, they're pulling their stomach in, and it makes the lungs smaller so they get a smaller breath.

Re-learning how you breathe totally shifts how you interact with the world because when you have shallow breathing, or reverse breathing, it pumps up the fear.

It's also something we do all the time, so it makes sense to invest in understanding more about the benefits of breathing properly. You can live without eating for days, but that's not the case with breathing. In terms of health, my prioritization is breathing is the most important, then water, then nutrition, then movement. I take that 80/20 approach and focus on the most important first. And even before breathing comes TLC (To the Light, Connect).

Animal Intuition

Animals are very good at picking up intuitive information. You can use this to get additional intuitive messages for your business.

Animals are psychic. There's a scientific study where people's pet dogs were home and the scientists sent the person on a random trip 50-100 miles away from home and they had a computer send off a pager message for the person to tell them they should start returning home.

They're videoing the dog, and the moment that person receives the page and they make the decision to return home, the dog changed his behavior, sitting by the front door to wait for them.

And it didn't hear the page, it didn't know what time the computer was picking.

They're more in tune with who they are and they don't question it. We question.

I believe that people are just as capable. There are stories of when a mother's son is killed in war, before she receives the telegram on the news, she woke up in the middle of the night and she just knew that her son had died. There's a psychic connection that people have, and we just generally don't pay attention to it.

Homeplay

- Pick one belief you have and play with changing it for a week-long experiment using one of the methods from this chapter. Notice how you feel not "wearing" this belief vs "wearing" it.

- Make a list of gratitudes for your intuition every day

- Go towards one of your smaller fears using TLC and WWIT. Treat it as an experiment.

- Practice intuiting who is calling on your phone or IMing you before you look at the name. Make a game of it.

Bonus Materials

The bonus materials from this chapter are at www.intuitiveleadershipmastery.com/bonus/

- Interview with Tal Gur (audio)

CHAPTER 3

Intuitive Hiring

"Intuition is the key to everything, in painting, filmmaking, business - everything. I think you could have an intellectual ability, but if you can sharpen your intuition, which they say is emotion and intellect joining together, then a knowingness occurs." - *David Lynch, director and author.*

Why Intuitive Hiring

You probably already use your gut instincts as part of your hiring process. In this chapter, we look at how you can ramp up that skill to make better and faster hiring decisions.

The problem often faced by business leaders in this arena is that traditional hiring can be a time and money sink, and there's no guarantee that spending those resources will result in you hiring the right person. And poor hires can cost you and your team even more time and money!

When I used to do hiring the "'logical" way, it took forever. I thought I had to go through every resume in detail and make pro/con lists and spreadsheets to try to figure out the best candidate to hire for every single position.

Now what I do instead is to get clear about who my ideal candidate is — what kind of skills and personality traits they need and so on. I'll take the list of candidates, and look for a "sticky" sensation. Either I'll feel down the list with my hand or let my eyes track above it, looking for the name where I sense a drag or impulse to stop, and I start with that person. Those are two ways to access selection. They just jump out.

I ask myself: WWIT (What Would It Take) for the ideal candidate to jump out at me? And soon enough they do. How this information comes to you depends on which way(s) you access your intuition. Some people are visual, some people hear stuff intuitively, some people feel it as they're more kinesthetic. Some people just get a "knowing."

A CEO at one of my workshops said about a recent hire:

> *"The person I hired stood out when I was looking through all the proposals. Hers was one that I immediately felt good about, but I felt like I still had to do a lot of testing with this candidate and other candidates to be satisfied (that) she was going to be the best ... And she was the best."*

This would be a great place to use an Intuition Journal (see Chapter 3) to write down something like "I had this first impression that Joan would be a great fit. Then I went through another four days of analysis and ended up hiring her as the best candidate."

If you don't feel comfortable making this decision without doing all of the other checking, then ask yourself a WWIT. What would it take for you to be comfortable making that decision without needing to do all the other analysis?

Perhaps you find a way to protect your downside if you do make a hiring screw-up. Accept that you are learning and playing with it — what's the worst that could happen? And how can you minimize the consequences? For example, you might give your chosen candidate a week's paid trial, with no obligation if things don't work out.

Eventually, starting the process by following your intuition can reduce stressful hiring by 90%. But initially you might chose to still go through your entire current hiring process while supplementing it with your new intuition skills.

Think of it as training wheels for your intuitive hiring skills. You didn't immediately learn to ride a bike the first time you got one. You had little training wheels. But after a while you learned to trust your ability to ride without them. It is the same with intuitive hiring. You use your intuition to pick an ideal candidate. You follow the process you use already. Then you compare the two. It is key to write down your intuitive information when you get it, because it's easy to forget these intuitive messages.

The following tools in this chapter are independent, and you can pick and choose which you want to play with adding to your hiring process first. There is no need to add all of them at once — just get used to adding them in one at a time!

True Costs of Poor Hiring

Have you considered what the true cost of just one bad hire is?

Incompetent staff don't just create a technical issue of poor work quality and missed deadlines, but they also tend to demoralize the other people on your team. Good workers will wonder why they should go the extra mile on doing good work when you hire and keep poor performers. They may also resent the sloppy worker leading to decreased team communication and output. Bad hiring can significantly increase turnover cost.

If you have to bring a new person into your team to replace someone else, you will pay for the learning curve and training time to bring them up to speed. This is a cost not only to the new person's time but also all the people who have to help him or her. In larger groups, there's a lot of time spent communicating between team members. Every time you change team members, it adds to your cost. And this is in addition to any direct hiring costs like staff interviewing time, advertising and recruiter fees!

There are also the lost opportunity costs of work you couldn't get done because you didn't have the staff in place to get the job done, and the cost of upsetting the good team members you have due to excessive workload.

Here are example costs of a bad hire in my company:

- Direct hiring costs $3,000

- Wasted training time for you and your team $10,000

- Lost management time $5,000

- Firing time and costs $6,000

- Risk that good staff on your team leave $10,000

- Lost opportunity cost $50,000

Total: $84,000

Michael Light

I don't know exactly what numbers you have on these bad hiring costs, and typically it is in the tens of thousands of dollars range, so you really want to avoid hiring any bad staff! This is even more true the higher the level the position you are hiring for (managers, VPs).

Because of the costs of a bad hire, my rule is:

If the candidate is not a "Hell Yes (hire)" then it is a "No hire." No maybes.

Are You Ready?

Are you ready for this change to your company of adding a new position or changing who does this job? Often a new hire won't go smoothly or will fail (quit or fired) because you have old patterns of self-sabotage in the way. If you notice any discomfort during the hiring process. then use the Youngest Age Pattern Recycle tool from Chapter 6 to clear it before you start your next hire.

Clear Intent - Your Ideal Candidate

Before you start asking your intuition for help on successfully filling your position, you must have super clear intent as to what you want and don't want.

- What is your ideal person for this position?
- What skills, characteristics and energy do they have?
  - Which ones must they have?
  - What ones would be nice to have?
  - What ones must they not have?

Your list of "Not haves" may be especially clear in your mind if you recently fired someone from the position who you thought would be a good fit but later turned out to be a disaster. Rephrase these negatives to the positive.

- Must not be a complainer → must have positive attitude
- Must not be late to meetings → is always on time to meetings

Note: Your ideal candidate may not be someone else's ideal candidate. Make your list unique to you, your business and the position.

Your intuition can help you in getting clarity by asking yourself WWIT (What Would It Take) to know what an ideal candidate is for me?

You may also draw on your own past experience with hiring and managing or the experience of other people you know who have been doing it for longer.

It may also come from perusing other people's job ads to find missing characteristics.

It may come from hiring several candidates for paid trial periods, not keeping them and repeating until you are clear what you want.

Why is clarity of your ideal candidate important? Because when you are clear, the WWITs work much better.

Example ideal candidate bullets for a marketing manager:

- You are a creative person who is passionate about implementing effective marketing campaigns.

- You are a genius at getting other team members to perform their best and beat their job metrics.

- You live and breathe GTD and get it all done on schedule every week.

- You love tasks to be organized and clear and change anything that is not to be that way pronto.

- You have a natural curiosity that drives you to learn, research and investigate.

- You have done some amazing work to date and are certain your best work is still ahead of you.

- You have an irrepressible joie de vivre that permeates your work and elevates it from good to great.

- You know that great marketing is the result of both your spiritual side and your practical side.

- You are good at working remotely, working smart for results and working reliably.

- You love to get results and track different marketing approaches obsessively to optimize your campaigns. You have a secret romance with numbers and statistics that makes this part of the job fun.

Are you an Ideal Candidate for Marketing Manager?

You see both the big picture of marketing goals (strategy) and can execute on the details (tactics) via a team. You love using and learning new marketing technology from CRMs to email marketing software. You are out of this world at getting results from other people doing the work details. You have organized marketing and managed people before, but not necessarily in the same position or the same way we do things.

WWIT to Attract An Ideal Candidate?

Now you are ready to use some WWITs (What Would It Take).

- WWIT to attract an ideal candidate?

- WWIT to attract an ideal candidate who can start by or before the end of this month?

As always with WWIT, you want to TLC (To the Light, Connect) first to get the best results. Then ask the question and see what inspired actions come to you. If you have resistance or blocks to this hire, you may need to ask the WWIT many times over several days to hear your intuitive answers.

You only need to hear the next step to take, not the whole plan and who you will hire.

For example: WWIT to attract an ideal marketing manager?

Inspired Actions:

- Posting a job ad in a certain job board

- Asking a friend for a referral

- Looking through your LinkedIn connections to see if someone jumps out at you

- Searching for that kind of person on LinkedIn.

- Who do I know in LinkedIn who is a marketing manager? If they are not available for this job, then who do they know?

- How could I use FB ads to find an ideal marketing manager?

- How can I have a better job ad than my competitors?

- What kind of salary will attract this person?

- Where do people like my ideal marketing manager hang out? Are there groups or conferences for them?

Start taking inspired actions and notice what candidates you are attracting.

WWIT For Your Job Ad to Stand Out?

As well as describing your ideal candidate, what the job consists of and what it would be like to work for your company, you want your job ad to stand out so that it attracts ideal candidates. Here are three ways to do this:

On a practical level, how you phrase the job and your company makes a big difference. You can go further by adding photos or a short video.

Whatever you do, it has to have energy. To understand what I mean, look at other companies' job ads. Browse a job site such as Monster or Craigslist and look at the job ads, but don't read them in detail. Just feel their energy. Some of them feel bright and shiny, like, "Wow! I'd like to work there." And some feel like, "Ugh, my god! What's going on here?"

Applicants may not be conscious of the job ad energy on a conscious level, but on their subconscious level, they get what energy you're putting out. So do some energy work to make your ad more bright and shiny.

Here are two ways to do that:

The first is to add light to your job ad. This will make it stand out to potential job applicants.

To do this, TLC yourself (To the Light, Connect from Chapter 1). Then TLC the job ad - imagine light coming from above and below into your job ad. Making it shine brightly and attract ideal candidates. It is the same process whether the ad is online or in a newspaper.

Tool: Meeting Magic

The second method is to use meeting magic on the ad.

Here is how. I am assuming that you already have an ideal candidate description and a good job ad.

- TLC (To the Light, Connect) yourself (see Chapter 1).

- Visualize a room. This is either your actual interview room or a virtual room where you will read resumes and talk with candidates on the phone.

- Put white roses in each corner to clear the energy of the room. (A rose is a spiritual symbol for pure energy).

- Put a rose by the door. Its job is to stop any bad candidate from getting in. Only ideal people are going to come into this room for the interview.

- Then list all the characteristics you want for this job hiring. For example:
  - Successful
  - Easy
  - Joyful

- ○ Whatever kind of experience you want this to be for you and the applicants. That's the intent you put into the meeting.
- • Visualize those words going into the room with light from above and below

While we use meeting magic for hiring, you can also use it for sales phone calls, deals, any type of place where you have to meet people or just regular meetings. You can do this so that it excludes unhelpful people from the meeting. And you set the intention as to what type of energy you want to come out of the meeting. Do you want a decision to be made in the meeting? Do you want people to be energized by it? Depends on what your intention is for the meeting.

Meeting Magic is from the book "What Do You Mean the Third Dimension is Going Away" by Jim Self

Use Gates and Delegated Process

If you do the shining of your light and attracting well, you may get inundated with candidates responding. It is not unusual to have hundreds of responses.

But remember that:

> **You only need to hire the first candidate that is a fit to your ideal list. No need to review all candidates.**

The faster you hire an ideal candidate, the faster they can join your team and you can make back the hiring costs in new opportunities. This is another benefit of getting crystal clear on your ideal candidate before you start your hiring.

One practical method to deal with a lot of applicants is to set up a series of gates that they must pass through. Your assistant checks the early gates and eliminates applicants who don't pass through those gates.

Here is an example Gate process that an assistant can follow:

Gate 1

1. Enter the name of everyone who responds into the spreadsheet with the first date we received information.
2. Then check to see if they followed instructions (in the job ad):
   a. Did they send a resume to us with a cover letter?
   b. Did they include links to their social media profiles? (It is OK if they don't have a profile on every network, but they need to have profiles on at least two.)
   c. Did they answer the Easter Egg questions in the job ad? (Easter Eggs are explained below.)
3. If they followed all instructions, enter a Y in the Gate 1 column. If not, enter an N and proceed to the next applicant.

Gate 2

1. Now evaluate the resume, cover letter/email and LinkedIn profile:
   a. Is their cover letter compelling?
   b. Do they have a track record of achievement? Do they typically exceed their goals?
   c. Do they have experience in the tasks in the job profile selling to an industry we want to target?
   d. Do they have experience selling to executives (VP level or higher)?

    e.   Have they sold near our price point? (Or did they make complex, high-ticket enterprise sales? Low-priced consumer sales?)

    f.   Are their cover letter, resume, and LinkedIn profile free of grammar, spelling, capitalization or punctuation errors?

2. Then check their other social media profiles:

    a.   Do they have good energy?

    b.   Do they understand how to use social media?

    c.   Do they treat their friends and others with respect?

    d.   Do they rant or do anything else that worries you?

You can find the full sample gates process document in the book bonus resources www.intuitiveleadershipmastery.com/bonus/

Easter Eggs

I often ask for an Easter Egg in the cover email. This is some simple piece of text that I request somewhere in the middle or end of the job ad.

An Easter Egg I have used with hiring cleaning staff is "Include your favorite color in the first sentence of your cover email." While you could use that question with any job ad, I tend to create easter eggs that tell me more about the person's ideal fit for the position.

For a marketing manager position, I used these two Easter Eggs:

- Start your cover message with "My favorite marketing method is" and tell us what it is and why?

- How do you develop and maintain your abundance mindset every day?

Those applicants who don't do this either didn't read the job ad fully or who don't pay attention to details. Out they go!

Of those who do answer the first Easter Egg question, I don't care what marketing method they mention — I am interested if they have passion for marketing and can write coherently.

The second question tells me if they have a spiritual way of looking at work and do they have a positive attitude. As that is part of my ideal candidate profile, this lets me eliminate bad fits fast.

Access Your Intuition to Save Time

When you are first using your intuition, it works best to give it extra material in the physical world to work with. Ask job applicants to provide a cover email, social media profiles or a handwriting sample. This will let you pick up more intuitive information on them.

It also lets you (or, better, your assistant) screen out bad fits using the Gates and Easter Egg processes above.

On a deeper intuitive level, if you have hundreds of applicants, you can pick out the most likely candidates quickly for a closer look. Just ask WWIT to find an ideal candidate fast? Then run your hand over a list of names (either on paper or on your computer screen) and mark the ones that feel "sticky." Alternatively, look over the list and see where your eye is drawn to. Mark those with colored text and you have saved beaucoup of hours of tedious work!

Now you are ready to evaluate your top few applicants more closely intuitively.

Two Chairs Method

TLC. Close your eyes and visualize yourself and your candidates in
chairs that are facing each other (the chairs, not necessarily the
people). You are the observer looking at you and the candidate on a
stage. Look at them in detail – are they facing you? Or angled towards
the stage? Or away from it? Is their head normal size, small or big? Do
they have legs and feet? What colors and emotions do you notice
about them? Any strange objects around them?

All of this provides intuitive information as to how good a fit they will
be. How grounded they are. If there are any hidden issues you should
be aware of. Interpret what you notice using your intuition. While
lack of feet in their image usually means not grounded in a particular
case, your intuition might be trying to tell you something else. Ask it
to find out.

You can either use this info as part of your hiring decision, or if you
have an otherwise good candidate with some minor issues, you can
send light to them to clear any problems. For example, grounding
them better. Or getting their attention on you.

Then re-evaluate the visualization to see if they responded favorably
or not.

Hiring Joy and Profit Graphs

For any applicant, you can use Joy and Profit Graphs to see how much
joy and profit they will bring to you over the years. Visualize each
graph in turn.

First the Joy Graph. Imagine how much joy do they bring you over
time as a graph. Is it a rising line? Does it go up and down? Does the
line suddenly end (they leave/fired)? The line goes downwards – an
energy draining employee

Some common possibilities for the graph are:

- On the up and up

- Line ends after so many months

- Up and down

- Downer

Do the same for Profit Graph.

Again, you can both read this intuitive information and if you have a candidate you otherwise like, you can send light using the TLC tool into the graph to fix any issues, for example, to make the joy start at a higher level, to avoid dips, to fix breaks in the line and to lengthen the number of joyful years you work together. After you have done your magic on the graph, check in with it again to see if it has changed how you want it. Some people are easy to shift, others are hardened cases that are not worth the amount of time and energy required to improve them.

Amazing Interviews

To have interviews go well, you can TLC (To the Light, Connect) yourself before the interview. And TLC the candidate. Go up and bring light down into them. Go down and bring light up into them. Expand their heart out as big as the universe.

Then visualize a line of light connecting your heart to their heart. When you have the interview, it's going to flow much more easily. I use this for job interviews on the phone or in person. I also use it for sales meetings. You can use it for any human interaction that you want to go well.

You don't have to tell them you're doing this. You are both going to feel better and perform better in the interview, making it more likely a good hiring decision will be made.

If you have multiple people involved in your interview process, then connect everyone to the light and to each other. For example, with three people you've got a triangle of light between their hearts so that they are all connected together.

With more people, the shape gets more complex, but you don't need to focus on the shape, just that you have commanded that the light connect all of them together.

Graphology for Weeding Out Bad Candidates

When I was starting out on intuitively reading candidates, I used a graphologist to read their personality info from their handwriting. Even asking candidates for a handwriting sample tended to filter out those who were not a fit for my company. Later I went to a graphology workshop and learned to read the signs from handwriting myself at an intermediate level.

If you are new to graphology, then one way to think about it is as micro body language. You probably know that you can tell a lot about a person from their body language and facial expressions – are they open or closed, confident or nervous, trustworthy or duplicitous.

Similarly, a person's personality and blocks comes out in their handwriting. If you have ever tried to change your handwriting, you will know that it is very deeply ingrained. It is very hard for even someone who knows what you are looking for to hide it in their handwriting. And it is impossible to do it in a way that cannot be detected because, to fake it, they have to write much slower than normal and you can see micro shaking in the writing – it just does not flow like normal writing.

Graphology for the Tablet Generation

Perhaps you are feeling hesitant to try graphology these days, especially for the "tablet generation" who don't do handwriting much. I asked a professional graphologist about this issue and here is what she said:

> "Graphology is absolutely invaluable even in a culture that types and prints. Everybody learns to write, and everybody has a signature. There are plenty of strokes (and personality traits) that can be discerned from placement on a page, spacing, and so on, even when looking at basic printing. Something as simple as a handwritten thank you note can be quite revealing.
>
> Also, in the signature alone, a wealth of information is revealed. The signature, which is our presentation to the world, often provides us with not only how the individual presents, but also the relationship with family, self-esteem, focus, transparency, anger issues, and communication style. In any context handwriting analysis can provide insight into the deeper or hidden traits that make a person who he or she is." - Raven Dana, graphologist

Typical issues to look for in handwriting include:

- All caps
- Letters not joined up

- Loops on y and g don't leave the lower zone
- Dotting I's and crossing T
- Where on the vertical Ts are crossed
- Loops and intersecting loops

If you want to interpret handwriting, either hire a professional graphologist or study a book on the subject. There are some suggestions in the Resources chapter at the end of this book.

Intuitive Offers

Now that you have selected an ideal candidate and had an amazing interview, you need to make an offer. How can you know the right amount of salary to offer someone?

Making job offers can be stressful. Will you offer too little and the candidate walks? Or offer too much and overpay?

The answer is to intuit what pay they will be happy with in this job for your company before you construct your offer and intuit what kind of negotiation style will leave them happy with the offer.

If it is a straight pay rate offer, you can ask your intuition what figure they will be happy with. "WWIT to know how much they will be happy with in this job?"

Or run your hand down a list of figures that represent potential offers and stop where the list feels sticky. Do this by having a list of possible salaries. Then feel down the list until it feels good or "sticky." You can also get this salary information in other ways (see the Advanced Intuitive Tools chapter for details).

When I have asked my intuition for the right salary offer, then I have successfully hired people with salaries that my ego didn't think they would take. I assume that they said inside something like "Wow! I really want to work for this company and this is a great opportunity." I don't know what went on in their head, but they said yes and have done great work for me and been happy about the job.

When you meet with the candidate to present the offer, you will get better results if you TLC and Heart connect to them during offer meeting/call. This is the same technique that we used during the interview stage and in the sales call process of Chapter 5. After all, what is hiring but you selling your company and the position/pay to the candidate and them selling you on hiring them?

You can also visualize all hearts connected – them, you, and the team they will work in. This makes for smoother on boarding.

Less Stress Next Time

Often managers wait until someone leaves or there is an urgent need to start the hiring process. This is stressful and makes it harder to access your intuition for a successful hire.

The answer is to "Always be hiring."

Every week ask yourself "WWIT (What Would It Take) to find an ideal candidate this week?"

Network with potential ideal candidates even when you don't have an open position. Be aware of people that stand out to you on LinkedIn. Listen to intuitive messages about the people you meet.

Keep in regular touch with the future ideal candidate and say that when you do have a position open you will call them. Your rolodex of potential future hires will reduce your stress next time you have to hire fast.

Playing with Intuitive Hiring Tools

If you don't fully trust yourself to use only intuitive tools at first, then add in one or more intuitive hiring methods to your existing process.

This gives you a safety net and provides reassurance that you are hearing your intuition correctly as you play and learn with it.

It is safe to explore the intuitive approaches because you'll still be drawing on whatever experience you have hiring in the traditional way.

Pick one of the intuitive methods and one of the traditional methods that are new to you to add to your next hiring.

Traditional hiring tools list

- Ideal candidate description
- Use gates and delegated process
- Easter Eggs

Intuitive hiring tools list

- WWIT to attract an ideal candidate?
- WWIT for your job ad to stand out?
- Two Chairs Method
- Hiring Joy and Profit Graphs
- Interview TLC

- Meeting Magic

- Graphology

- Intuitive offers

It is ok to use whatever combination of traditional and intuitive hiring methods that work for you at this moment in your intuition learning.

Homeplay

- Write down a bullet point list of your ideal candidate.

- WWIT to attract an ideal candidate? Write down inspired actions and do them.

- Create a Gate process for hiring, including Easter Eggs.

- Play with using one of the intuition methods to find ideal candidates from the list of applicants faster.

Bonus Materials

The bonus materials from this chapter are at www.intuitiveleadershipmastery.com/bonus/

- Sample Gates Hiring document (doc)

- Interview about Hiring with Mads Singers (audio)

- Interview about Hiring with Neil Napier (audio)

CHAPTER 4

Intuitive Decisions

"Good instincts usually tell you what to do long before your head has figured it out." — *Michael Burke, CEO of Louis Vuitton*

Why decide intuitively

I ntuitive decision-making is more important now than ever before. The speed of business has increased a lot in the last few years, and information overload is at an all-time high. Intuition can save you lots of time over a complete rational analysis. Faster decisions means you can beat your competition, become profitable faster and be less stressed, too.

In the previous chapter, we looked at intuitive hiring and how that can cut through the myriad of information on possible job applicants to let you hire ideal candidates faster.

In this chapter, we look at a close decision to make on hiring in more detail with ten different decision-making methods ranging from the super logical to the fully intuitive.

Why do we even need decision methods? If one job applicant sucked and the other was brilliant, it would be easy — pick the brilliant one!

But often there are two or more options that are really close and it is hard to decide which is best. And the ramifications of a bad decision could be thousands of dollars of extra cost, a failed project and weeks of wasted work.

Often those of us with a strong "Protestant work ethic" make the work of deciding harder than it has to be — things don't have to be hard to be effective! Sometimes the easy option is right in front of us, but we choose something that is more difficult because we are conditioned that "hard work is the best work."

Just for a moment, suspend your prior beliefs on how you should approach decision-making.

We will look at some common methods of how to make intuitive decisions below. But first let's hear from Rob, CEO of a publishing company, about how he went from purely logical decisions to using more intuition.

"Gut instinct is something I ignored for a long time, trying to force myself to work only on the numbers. I've since learned that even when the numbers work, you still need to check your gut. This lesson was taught through two experiences.

The first came from reading a post on the Farnam Street blog called "How Using a Decision Journal Can Help You Make Better Decisions."

Summary: When you make a decision, write down the details of your decision and what you expect to happen.

The second punch in the combo came as I was rifling through Evernote on an international flight. The search term I used brought up a journal entry from around a year and a half earlier, where I'd noted down some gut feelings about a situation...

Before promptly bulldozing over them in pursuit of my goal.

It was like having a weight loss before / after in front of me. The gut instinct had been right, I'd ignored it, and paid the price for bulldozing."

On to the common decision methods from totally logical to pure intuition. Hopefully these will help you to avoid "paying the price for bulldozing" in the future.

The pros and cons list

List out the pros (benefits) and cons (drawbacks) of each choice. Pick the one with most benefits and least drawbacks. Let's stay with the hiring example to illustrate this.

Applicant A

Pros	Cons
Prior experience in this field	Cannot start for a month
Passion for the project	Higher salary requirement
Extra skills beyond what we currently need	

Applicant B

Pros	Cons
Lots of experience in the industry	Needs to relocate
Has managed others successfully	
Ready to start immediately	
Brings a large list of useful contacts with her	

In this case, B has more pros than A and less cons, so it is the best choice using the pros/cons method.

Weighted Pros and Cons

This is the same as the previous pros/cons method, but gives each aspect of the choice a weight depending on how important it is. Pros get a weighting of +1 to +10 and the cons a weighting of -1 to -10, depending on how good or bad they are. Multiply the score by the weight and add them up. Pick the option with the most positive score.

For example, in hiring, database design might be an important factor in choosing a candidate, with a weighting of 3. Candidate A has a database design score of +5. Candidate B has a score of -2. So the contribution for A is 3 x 5 = 15 and for B is 3 x (-2) = -6. Add these to the weighted scores for all other aspects of your decision to get the total scores.

Here is an example of a job candidate scoring with 3 weighted items. (In a real job search, you might have 10-20 items.)

Candidate A

	Weight	Score	Weighted score
Database design	3	+5	15
Indents code	1	+6	6
Dresses smartly	1	-2	-2
Total			19

Candidate B

	Weight	Score	Weighted score
Database design	3	-2	-6
Indents code	1	+5	5
Dresses smartly	1	+3	3
Total			2

In this example, A's score of 19 beats B's score of 2

Tip: I give extra weight to an item that is easily reversible, gives early feedback on whether it is the right course, or can be corrected down the road.

Particular areas I have found the weighted pro/con method useful for are:

- Scoring job candidates on the different skills and characteristics in the job requirement.

- Scoring clients by "idealness" (such as how easy they will be to work with, whether their salary fits the budget for this role, if they communicate clearly, appreciate the quality of work that we do, etc.) and then "firing" the bottom 10% of clients each year.

- Scoring prospects the same way, focusing my energy on the top-scored prospects, and then eliminating the bottom scores as "not a fit."

Flip A Coin

If the choices are nearly equal, it doesn't matter. Pick one at random. Then see how you feel about the decision.

If you feel good, great— go with it. If you get a bad feeling in your stomach, then you know it's not the right choice, and you can pick the other one! (You just realized new information about the first choice.)

This method has the additional advantage that is fast to do. And in business, fast decisions are better than slow ones (see section below).

Test Them Out With A Trial

Hire the different top candidates for a few hours or a week of paid work to see how you get on and what they really can do. Use the extra interactions with them and your team to give you more information on how they would be working full time for your company.

Bring the Choices to Your Heart

When a decision is pretty equal and complex, then using intuition can help. Your intuition processes all the complexity at a subconscious level, thereby saving your conscious processing power for other thoughts. It is also fast to do.

This is one method for making intuitive decisions, or at least giving you extra info for your conscious decision process.

Let's say you're making a decision between 4 different options.

- Drop down into your heart (imagine your consciousness is in an elevator from your head).

- Hold each of options 1 - 4 in your hand one at a time.

- Bring your hand to your heart and notice what you feel.

- Then bring one more option into the mix: something else that you don't consciously know right now to your heart, too.

- Pick the option that makes your heart feel most open and happy.

- Notice any extra info you get on each option (e.g., heart feels heavy, a color or sound that appear, other body sensations, new inspired thoughts that come to you).

- If you get the "Something else" option, then be patient a few days and see what occurs to you or synchronicities that occur that point to what it is.

(Exercise from the book "Beyond Human." by Jaden Phoenix)

Ask for Intuitive Signs

You can ask your intuition to give you signs to help make a decision or to confirm you have made the right decision. Ask yourself "WWIT (What Would It Take) to know the ideal decision for me for ___?" Fill in the blank for the question you are deciding on.

You might get the information in different ways:

- Words come into your head. It might be the name of one of the choices, or a characteristic that it has or perhaps a perceptive question you need to ask yourself about the choice.

- A 'knowing' that a certain choice is true for you. By a knowing, I mean you just know it is true. The same way when you say "My name is ____ (your name)," you know it is true, whereas if you said another name, it would feel false to you.

- Animal signs (see Animal Symbols section in Chapter 9, Advanced Intuitive Tools, for more details.)

- Messages from dreams (see more on this below).

Dreams and WWIT

It is easier to access your intuition in dreams or in the just-woken state of mind, because the ego part of the mind is quieter then. To get answers from your intuition in dreams, you can ask yourself before sleep, "WWIT (What Would It Take) to know the ideal decision for me for ___?" Fill in the blank for the question you are deciding on. E.g., "WWIT to know the ideal decision for hiring my marketing manager?"

Make sure that you have a pen, a pad of paper and a small flashlight by your bed, because dreams or thoughts on waking can be hard to remember even a few minutes later. You want to write them down as soon as you are awake, either in the middle of the night or first thing in the morning. Write clearly enough so that you can read it later when you are fully awake.

You might get clear words or images on what to do, or you might get messages in images that you will need to interpret. You may need to do this for several nights in a row to get answers. But as it only takes an extra minute to ask the WWIT before sleeping, there is no great difficulty in adding this into your evening routine.

Joy and Profit Graphs

You can visualize Joy and Profit Graphs for each option (plus the something else option that you don't consciously know). See Chapter 3 on Hiring for details.

Ask Your Future Self

Your future self already knows which decision gave him or her the most joy or profit. Why not ask them for advice?

To do this, get in a quiet place and imagine your future self in front of you. Then ask them which option gave them the best result. You can clarify "best" by asking for which gave the most joy, the most profit, the most success.

For more details, see Chapter 8, Visioning.

Ask Angels and Guides

Ask one of your angels or guides who is best able to help with this decision to come in front of you. Ask them which option gives the "best" result for you. You might hear an answer or receive a sign or just get a deep knowing on the answer. You can ask them or anyone else you like in your Spiritual Advisory Board (see Chapter 1 for details of this).

Other Intuitive Decision Methods

There are many other ways to access your intuition. I encourage you to play with the different methods and pick the options that work for you.

Other methods include:

- Tarot cards

- Pendulum

- Picking rune dice from a bag

- Animal signs

Hidden Decision Factors

We talked about common decision methods above, including intuition. Here are two further thoughts on close decisions:

The Time Value of Decisions

The values of the different options are usually not fixed over time. Often they decline over time. In addition, the days and energy you spend making a decision are time and energy you could have spent on other productive tasks in your business, so they have a cost, too.

Either don't wait to decide, or make a conscious decision to decide later! No more worrying about a decision for days and losing time and energy unnecessarily.

For example, in hiring, the slower you are at responding to the different candidates, the less enthusiastic they will be about the job, and the more likely they are to pick another company, plus the more time you have lost for other money-making tasks.

If you have done the intuitive decision exercises and have a clear sense of who the right candidate is, you don't need to worry about rushing into a wrong hire. Your intuition will guide you through the process, and even if it doesn't work out, you will have wasted less time and resources than if you spent weeks and weeks looking at every detail.

Example: Suppose you have two candidates, A and B, with weighted pros/cons score values of 51 and 49 on Day 1 and that they lose 3 points each day you wait. It costs 3 points in your energy used each day.

Here are the values of the options over time:

Day	A	B	N
1	51	49	-30
2	48	46	-33
3	45	43	-36

(Column N represents making No decision — see section below on lost opportunity cost for explanation of this.)

In this case, making a fast "bad" decision on Day 1 by hiring B at 49 points is actually better than the slow "correct" decision of hiring A on Day 3 at 45 points.

True, sometimes the value of the choices might not change over time, but the cost of continuing to spend your time and energy on the decision day after day definitely applies. This is time that could have been spent making money for your business other ways. There is always a time cost to a decision.

The only way to avoid that is to not worry about the decision or spend any time on it at all until you next consider the choice — a deliberately delayed decision. I have seen entrepreneurs successfully do this when they realize that they are too busy or lack resources to implement another change this year and "consciously decide not to decide" until next January.

Lost Opportunity Cost

I also did not include the lost opportunity cost of a delayed decision. This includes all the profits and new deals you could have made in the days (weeks?) spent decision-making using either choice A or B.

We are not just comparing choice A to B, but also to choice N — do nothing. In the case of a 49/51 near equal decision, I imagine the value of N is much less than either A or B. It is often negative.

In sales, often clients don't take the cost of choice N into account because they have had the problem and been in this choice for so long. It is my job, when wearing my salesperson hat, to help them see the true costs of choice N, as well as the costs and benefits of choosing to buy from me. This helps to bring more consciousness to their buying decision.

Intuition journal

To improve both your intuition and decision-making abilities, I recommend you keep an intuition journal.

This can either be a paper journal or a spreadsheet of decisions made. For each decision write down:

- the date
- all the options you considered
- what your gut was saying about each of them and
- which one was your final choice and why

Review your intuition journal monthly to see how things worked out. This will let you see where your intuition was trying to tell you something but you did not hear. As Rob learned in the story in the introduction to this chapter, ignoring your intuition and bulldozing through another option may not work out well.

Case Study - Tal's Travel Decisions

When Tal Gur left his home for the first time in his 20s, he didn't have a plan. He told me that he remembered looking at the wall map of the world and feeling frightened.

It was scary because, before, he always had some kind of a plan. For the first time when looking at the wall map, he didn't know where to go. Because he could go anywhere, nowhere was the next clear place. (He has an online business that can support him anywhere.)

In order to think about the decision and recover from the debilitating illness he had in the stressful cubicle job he had quit, he decided to go to Israel for two weeks to visit his family. That illness which had been going on for month, the back pains, everything disappeared. Suddenly, he started to get clarity. For example, he had a list of 100 life goals (a "bucket list"). One of the items was learning to dance salsa. He said, "All right, I'm going to dance salsa in Colombia, I'm going to fly to Colombia and dance salsa. That feels right."

He had been looking through his list, and this one item felt right. He could not explain it logically.

He told his family, "I'm going to dance salsa in Colombia," and they said, "Well, you can dance salsa here in Israel, why fly all the way to Colombia?" He told them it felt right, and that intuitively he knew that Colombia was where he needed to go. Since then, he told me, following his intuition has really helped him.

This is a good intuition decision technique that Tal used: Picking an item from a list by feeling with your intuition. It might be a list of different options, a list of different prospects to call, a list of different places you might travel to, or different products you might launch. Feeling through the list of which one feels right is a way to hear your intuition's message.

The key is being open to what you might hear. Tal was open so he could actually hear his intuition.

If you are too much in your mind, you would look at the list and might not see or hear the right choice. You might be open to hearing your intuition, but you need to get out of your mind, connected to your body, to make it easier to connect to your intuition.

This is important because we tend to tune out. Intuition is often a quiet voice, and it's easy to turn up the music in our mind, just like if you're in a car and you have a GPS, you can hear the turn left, turn right messages unless you have cranked up the radio, in which case you don't hear any directions.

Intuition is a bit like a GPS: It gives us guidance, but you have to listen to hear it. It's up to us to decide whether we want to take the guidance or not.

Before this episode, Tal was always logical, he didn't believe in intuition, he always tried to explain, understand, put boundaries, put labels, definitions, and control things. That is what the mind wants, to control our reality, but for Tal, now it's different. Now he listens.

Tips for Better Intuition Decisions

Calm Mind

First, calm your mind to access your intuition (rather than hearing your ego). Meditation, walking in nature or even taking a shower can calm your mind. Deep, slow breathing helps if you can do the previous activities (10 seconds per inhale and 10-20 seconds per exhale for a few minutes is good for this purpose).

Tool: Going Low

You can also calm your mind by Going Low. To do this imagine your consciousness is in an elevator in your head and take it down. Go down through your through your throat, your chest, your tummy, until your consciousness is in your hips. Notice how quiet your mind is now and also how quiet your emotions are. This is a method I learned from Mark Dunn. See the Resources Chapter for more details on Mark.

Fear Vs Love

Second, ask yourself if you are taking a decision based on fear or on love. How to tell?

It is based on fear when your emotions around the decision are fear-driven. You could ask yourself, "What if I don't pick this option, how do I feel?" For example, suppose you have a project that you really, really want to happen and your inner thoughts are "I'm afraid that X might happen," then you are taking the decision based on fear and not on love.

If you were deciding to do that project based on love, then you would do it because it really resonates with who you are and the other tasks that you are doing.

If you are only looking at the numbers and data to try to see if it makes sense to do something, then that is a decision based on fear. When Apple created the iPod, they did not analyze endless numbers and marketing focus groups. They had a vision from the CEO's intuition.

Get Out Of The Problem Space

You cannot take a successful decision in the same space as the problem comes from. Often the whole energy of the problem space is full of other people's thoughts and worries about the issue. Then it is hard to hear your intuition provide solutions.

If you are finding it hard to make a decision in a particular case, then I recommend getting outside away from other people and moving your body. That frees you from other people's energy and your anxiety. This is why going for a walk when you have a problem often leads to flashes of inspiration that give you a solution.

Relaxing or taking your mind off the problem also helps. That is why asking "WWIT (What Would It Take) to solve this problem?" before a nap or sleep at night can give you the solution when you wake.

Ego Vs Intuition

How do you know the answer comes from your intuition and it's not just part of your ego telling you? How do you tell the difference?

The first thought (within 3 seconds) is intuition. Later thoughts are second guesses from ego or from influence of society or friends.

When a decision comes from your ego, then it's generally related to fear. The ego wants to keep things safe and may act defensively of itself. The ego is afraid of the risk of us failing, it doesn't want us to be embarrassed in front of other people. It is full of doubts.

The intuition comes from trust and higher truth. It doesn't have any doubts. You just know the action is the right thing to do for you in this time. When you don't have doubts, it's because your higher self is saying, "That's what you need to do."

Hearing Your Inner Voice Vs Others

What about if you have other people's expectations or other people's energies around this decision? How do you access your intuition in that case? How can you clear that out before you listen to yourself so you're not hearing other people's answers?

Many leaders are natural empaths and pick up what people around them feel. It is good to understand how other people's energy can affect us and having that awareness and to connect with yourself. This is where clearing your aura comes into play.

Clearing Your Aura

To get clarity on what your own intuition is saying, clear your aura. Getting other people's energy out of your aura lets you hear your inner-self better.

In case you are not familiar with the aura, it is the energy field around you that contains your energy and the energy of other people you have interacted with. It's an extension of your physical body to the space around you — your energy body. It is what lets you be aware of someone staring at you without you seeing them.

Ideally your aura would only contain your energy, but the truth is that we are always interacting and exchanging energy with others.

To clear your aura, you can start by being alone, quiet your mind and get into silence. Be in a place far away from other people and electronics. Connect with your body. Use one of those relaxation exercises where you go through each part of the body in turn and notice what you feel in each part.

You can download a progressive relaxation audio from the bonus materials at www.intuitiveleadershipmastery.com/bonus/

Once you start noticing the sensations and emotions in your body parts, then it is easier to recognize your energy field (the aura), too. You might have some sort of vision or hear something or just sense it.

Golden Rose Aura Vacuum Cleaner

As you notice negative energy in your body or aura, you can use a golden rose to suck out the negative stuff. Visualize a big gold rose in front of you. It is like an aura vacuum cleaner that will suck all the energy that is not yours. Ask it to release any kind of energy that is not yours, just let it go.

Then visualize on top of your head a gold and shiny sun, which is your higher self. Let it illuminate yourself completely with your own energy. All the other energies, put into the vacuuming golden rose.

You can also use this method when you have a headache or if something is worrying you a lot, because headaches and worry are often stored in the aura rather than the physical body. Just visualize throwing the headache or worry into your golden rose. Then when you feel it is done, throw the rose to infinity and see it exploding to release the energy you removed.

Salt Baths for Clearing

On a practical level, you can clean your aura by taking a salt bath. Add 1-3 cups of salt to a bath and relax in it for 10-20 minutes. You can use regular table salt, table salt plus bicarbonate of soda, or use Epsom salts. If you have not tried this before, you may be surprised how good you feel afterwards, and how much more "yourself" you feel.

You can leave your head out of the water if you prefer, though pulling your head under the salt water will clear stuck energy in your head faster. (I do admit, it can make your hair feel a bit rough afterwards.) After the bath, rinse off the salt water with a short shower.

You probably have experienced the feeling of wellbeing you get at the seaside, especially if you swim in the sea, which, of course, is salt water. Even walking along the beach and paddling your feet in the salt water feels good.

You can speed up and make the salt water clearing more powerful by visualizing that your physical and energy bodies are getting clean. Everything that is not yours is dissolving away into the water, and the sea is just taking everything away.

Spending time by and in the sea combines the benefit of being in nature and cleaning your aura with water. The ocean has a lot of power — it can also really empower us.

If you are not near the ocean or don't have a bath, then a shower can also clean your aura. You can rub salt scrub over your body to add in the salt that a salt bath would have provided.

Play With the Tools

When you next have a decision, in addition to your regular decision method, play with one of the other methods from this chapter and compare results in your Intuition Journal. Then a month or two later compare how the decision worked out with what you noted down from each method. This will help you build your trust in the new methods or suggest modifications.

- The pros and cons list
- Weighted pros and cons
- Flip a coin
- Test them out with a trial
- Bring the choices to your heart
- Ask for intuitive signs
- Dreams and WWIT
- Joy and Profit Graphs
- Ask your future self
- Ask Angels and Guides

Homeplay

- Play with one of the intuitive decision methods this week (maybe in addition to your current method).

- Play with one of the aura cleaning methods and notice how that affects your decision-making ability.

- Start an Intuition Journal or spreadsheet of decisions made and what your gut was saying about them. Review it monthly to see how things worked out.

Bonus Materials

The bonus materials from this chapter are at
www.intuitiveleadershipmastery.com/bonus/

- Progressive relaxation meditation (audio)
- Connect with your Future Self (audio)

CHAPTER 5

Intuitive Sales

"I always did something I was a little not ready to do. I think that's how you grow. When there's that moment of 'Wow, I'm not really sure I can do this,' and you push through those moments, that's when you have a breakthrough." – *Marissa Mayer, CEO of Yahoo*

The Problem with Traditional Sales Methods

T raditional sales is a numbers game. You contact a lot of prospects, and a certain percentage buy. It is a logical approach to deal with the uncertainty of not knowing ahead of time who is ready to buy.

The "numbers approach"' makes sales a grind because you have to make so many sales calls that end in no sale. And most prospects have a lot of resistance to being sold to in the traditional way, which often makes your numbers worse.

In a traditional sales meeting, you may follow a sales process for dealing with objections and closing. For example, you might follow steps to make your prospects "Know, Like and Trust" you during your sales process, but it can be draining dealing with the constant rejection.

Intuition gives you a more efficient way.

Instead of following traditional sales steps to move the prospect up a ladder of Know, Like, Trust until they Buy, Repeat, Refer, what if you moved them directly on an energetic level? What if you could build an energetic connection with them and determine if a sale was likely ahead of time without all the traditional sales work?

What if you could just have your prospects trust you immediately?

Or to put it another way: what if you could pick the prospects who are energetically connected to you already and make them an offer first? We will learn how to do this below.

Ideal Client Attraction

Before you can successfully energetically attract your ideal clients, you need to get super clear on who they are and what they are like.

Why? Because this lets your intuitive mind work more efficiently to bring the right connections to you.

What kind of company are they? What titles do they have? What characteristics should they have?

Here is an example of an ideal client for the custom software business that I own. The client should...

- Have 50+ employees so we know they can afford our services

- Understand software development process and want to follow best practices

- Be comfortable having us work with CIO or other C-level executives who can make decisions fast

- Pay promptly and accept bills cheerfully

- Fun to work with

- Appreciates working with us

- Communicates clearly and at an appropriate frequency

- Give us referrals to new clients

- Have clear requirements already (or be willing to pay us to create them)

You might take this a step further and create an ideal client avatar – an imaginary client together with their backstory and photo.

Here is an example of one of this book's avatars:

Primary: CEO

- Perspective
  - They want to grow their company, but don't want to work even more hours or get more stressed.
  - They are open to intuition and spiritual methods
  - They are a successful CEO that has good business intuition for doing deals, hiring, sales and getting teams motivated... but are keeping it private, believing that:
    1) your intuition skill level is what you were born with and

2) it cannot be improved?

- Capability fit
  - Deep experience with business intuition - both in my own companies and coaching others.
- Profit potential
  - Yes if they own a company with 10+ staff, they can afford to invest in growing their company using intuition

Background:

- What is this person's experience in this industry?
  - 10+ years
- What are they responsible for?
  - Company vision, growth, probably sales
- What is the profile of their company (revenue, headcount, trajectory)
  - $2MM, 10+ staff, growing
- Demographic:
- Age, gender
  - Female, 40
- Income
  - $150k+
- Family status
  - divorced

- Location
  - San Francisco, California

You can find the rest of this avatar and other avatar examples in the bonus section of the website www.intuitiveleadershipmastery.com/bonus/

I hope you're starting to see the pattern here. It is similar to what we did in Hiring and Marketing chapters. You clarify what your ideal client is. Then use WWIT (What Would It Take) and other intuition tools to evaluate and attract them.

WWIT to Find Your Ideal Clients?

Now that you know clearly who your ideal client is, it is time to ask your intuition for help to find them. As always, first TLC (To the Light, Connect) then ask yourself:

- WWIT to find my ideal clients?

You may get immediate inspired actions to take. Or if you have blocks to hearing your intuition, you may need to ask the question several times over a few days.

An inspired action will be a next step that gets you nearer to your ideal clients. For example:

- Call Bob (an old client) and ask for referrals
- Try out that prospecting method that you read about last year
- Go to a certain networking event or meeting
- Go to lunch at a certain restaurant (but you don't know why)

Sometimes it is clear that the action will likely get you some ideal clients. Other times you may need to trust your intuition that it will work out in the end. The lunch example above is one of those. Perhaps you will meet someone there who introduces you to an ideal client. Or perhaps you will see some news there that takes you to the next step. The more experience you have of trusting intuitive nudges and the results they can bring, the more you will listen to them and act immediately on them. And the more you act on them, the more you will notice them.

Other times you may get an answer from your intuition, but you don't know how to achieve that next step. That is the time to use Nested WWITs (see Chapter 1 for details) Here is an example:

- WWIT to find my ideal clients?
    - IA: create a video about their pain
    - WWIT to create a video about their pain?
        - IA: Find a great videographer in town
        - WWIT to find a great videographer in town?
- IA: search my LinkedIn for video.

[WWIT = What Would It Take
IA = Inspired Action]

In this example, we kept asking WWIT at each level until we got to an Inspired Action that we knew how to do and could do it now.

Feeling Lists of Who to Contact

Instead of contacting everyone on a prospect list, why not ask your intuition to help find the ones who are ready to buy now? Have the list in front of you, either on paper or your screen. TLC, then ask yourself:

- WWIT to find prospects who are ready to buy from me now?

Then either close your eyes and feel with your hand along the list until it feels sticky, or run your eyes with a soft gaze over the list until they are attracted to a certain line.

Either way, highlight that line and keep moving until you have gone through the entire list.

Then for each prospect your intuition found, ask yourself:

- WWIT to easily and successfully connect with this person today?

And follow the inspired action you get. (It might be email, phone, ask a friend for an introduction, Twitter PM or other)

Intuitive LinkedIn

This method also works on LinkedIn. The list might be the result of a search for prospects you have run or a page of "suggested people you might know" that LinkedIn shows you. Again, you feel or look for the "sticky" people on the list and WWIT to connect to them.

In traditional sales, you would use that as preparation so you could talk about points in common. But intuitively, you can pick up someone's energy from their profile, so that can tell you objections they might have or how to best approach them. Ask:

- WWIT to connect with this person in way most likely to lead to a future sale?

How to Have Prospects Come to You

I love it when ideal prospects come easily to me. Here are two ways you can work on this:

Abundance Tree

The abundance tree is a powerful spiritual tool for growing your business. Here is the visualization below. There is a recording of this in the book bonus resources page at www.intuitiveleadershipmastery.com/bonus/

Close your eyes. TLC (To the Light, Connect - see Chapter 1 for details on how to do this).

Then imagine you are walking in a forest. You come to a sunny clearing. It's all peaceful and beautiful there. There is your business's abundance tree in the middle of it. Examine it from bottom to top. How are the roots? The Trunk? The branches and leaves? How is the fruit? What kind of tree is it? Are there people, animals or birds around it? How are they behaving? What emotions do you notice when you are with your abundance tree?

Are there any issues with this tree, such as small roots, flat trunk, missing sections, weird colors or energy?

Ask your intuition what these issues mean in your business.

Any area of the tree you want to improve, send light from above and below to it. Ask WWIT for it to be better?

See the tree bringing you a regular supply of ideal clients and projects. See it bringing you profits and joy. Feel gratitude towards it. Thank it for what it brings you.

I recommend spending about a minute per day on this visualization.

After doing this for a few weeks, you will start to notice more ideal clients easily coming to you.

In a workshop, we did the abundance tree visualization and one of the CEOs noticed that:

> *"For some reason, I immediately went to this conversation I just had with a client, and as soon ... She is such an ideal client, and as soon as I told her the price, she just so shut down, and I essentially just got basically what I wish I would have said to her right there."*

You may get inspirations from this meditation. You might get that your tree's branches are good, but the roots are small. Meaning that there's something in your business that's not supporting it quite right.

Attracting Star Field

TLC. Visualize the night sky with millions of stars. Each star represents a person or company that you might work with. Some of the stars are your ideal clients. Some are not. See the ideal client stars twinkling and brighter than the other stars. Bring them nearer to you. Like if you had fishing lines to each of them and you are pulling them in. Experience gratitude for so many ideal clients coming to you so easily.

There is nothing else to do unless you get inspired actions for how to bring these clients to you. If you are afraid it is not working, I recommend reviewing Chapter 2, especially the sections on learning to increase trust in your intuition.

Intuitive Pricing

Here is a heart-based approach to price setting.

If you have a service, pick a dollar number per hour or day for your rate. If you have a product, pick a price for it. Then:

- on a scale of 0-10, how comfortable are you with charging that amount? (0 = totally comfortable, 10 = shit scared)

Adjust your price number up or down until you are at a 7 comfort level. That way, you are stretching yourself just enough for where you are in your business now.

This is not a one-time activity. After a few months at the price, you may find yourself more comfortable with it than a 7, in which case, repeat the exercise. You can test out the new price on new prospects.

Secondly, how much money do you want to receive for a day of consulting work where you can feel "Hell, yes, I love doing this"? Make sure you are charging at least this amount.

Attracting Prospects to Your Website or Location

How your website or business physical location feels affects how many prospects you can attract or keep in your sales cycle. You can, of course, hire a designer to make things look clean and organized in the physical world (or online). But what I am talking about here is changing the energy of your business website and location.

Making it feel inviting and inspiring trust to those who enter.

First, TLC. Then feel the energy in different parts of your website or location. Where does it feel friendly and trustworthy? Where is it neutral? Where does it feel negative or yucky? Then use one of the energy clearing methods from Chapter 1 to shift the negative parts. For example, you can TLC your website by imagining it is in front of you and light coming into it from above and below, clearing away the negative energy.

Evaluating Leads

So you have found a prospect, but how can you tell if they are worth meeting with? What is the probability of a sale and for how much? Also, if they do buy, will they be an ideal client or the client from hell?

In traditional sales, you might look at various qualifying items to decide if you want to meet with a prospect:

- Size of their company

- Their job title

- How much pain you think they have

- Whether they have paid a fee to meet with you

- Whether they have bought other products or services from you in the past

Here are two intuitive methods that can give you extra information *before* you take the time to meet with them. (These methods are the same as the ones I showed you in the Intuitive Hiring chapter but applied to the sales situation. After all, in hiring, you are selling the candidate on working for your company, so it is very similar to having prospects buy from you).

Two Chairs Method

TLC. Close your eyes and visualize yourself and them in chairs that are facing each other (the chairs, not necessarily the people). You are the observer looking at you and the prospect on a stage.

Look at them in detail – are they facing you? Or angled towards the stage? Or away from it? Is their head normal size, small or big? Do they have legs and feet? What colors and emotions do you notice about them? Any strange objects around them?

All of this provides intuitive information as to how ideal a client they will be for your company. How grounded they are. If there are any hidden issues you should be aware of.

You can either use this info as part of your meeting decision, or if you have an otherwise good prospect with some minor issues, you can send light to them to clear any problems. For example, grounding them better by TLCing them or getting their attention on you by shining light from your heart to their heart.

Then re-evaluate the visualization to see if they responded favorably or not.

I did the two chairs method in a workshop with a CEO and here is what occurred:

- How does the other person appear to you?
  - Really happy and, like, loving.
- Can you see their head?
  - Yes.
- Can you see their feet?
  - Yes.
- Are they looking directly at you, or are they looking off to somewhere else?
  - They're looking away from me (the observer), like they are distracted.

- Send them light from above and below. Visualize a cord of light connecting them to you. Now where are they looking?
  - They are looking directly at me now.
- Anything else about them you notice?
  - They are confident in me.

It might seem that you need to have met this prospect in person before you can use the two chairs method. That is not the case.

You only need to connect with them energetically. A good way to do that is to go to their social media profile: LinkedIn, Facebook, Twitter or some other profile. That will give you their energy to connect to for this process.

And on a practical level, this is a good sales tip anyway. When you are prospecting, always look at people's social media profiles. You will get all kinds of information from there.

- Are they are a nice person in comments with other people, or are they are a bit of a prick?
- Do they bother to spell things right in their social media posts?
- What are they interested in?

Those are the physical things, but you also get energy of the person. You just look at their profile quickly and notice what impressions you pick up.

A veteran salesperson I know can look at LinkedIn profiles and within 5 seconds they get a gut feeling if that person is an ideal client or not and an inspired action to take to make a sale come closer.

Joy and Profit Graphs

For any prospect you can use joy and Profit graphs to see how much joy and profit they will bring to you over the years. Visualize each graph in turn. First the Joy Graph. How much joy do they bring you over time? Is it a rising line? Does it go up and down? Does the line suddenly end (they stop buying from you or you fire them for bad client behavior)?

Some of the different possibilities include:

- On the up and up

- Line ends after so many months

- Up and down

- Downer

Do the same for Profit Graph.

Again, you can both read this intuitive information, and if you have a prospect that you otherwise like, you can send light into the graph using TLC to fix any issues, for example, to make the joy start at a higher level, to avoid dips, to fix breaks in the line and to lengthen the number of joyful years you work together. After you have done your magic on the graph, check in with it again to see if it has changed how you want it. Some prospects are easy to shift, others are hardened cases that are not worth the amount of time and energy required to improve them!

This is all information from your intuition. You might have problems with them, or they might leave after two years. Or you might have to invest in them for a certain period of time before you see a return come back. You can get a lot of information in this way that can reduce your sales time and increase results.

Here is an example from a CEO in a workshop that I gave:

- Pick a new client that you might choose to work with. Visualize what does the Profit Graph look like from this client? Is it like straight up, is it wiggly, are there gaps in it? Does it go up and down? Does it not start anywhere? What does it look like? What's the Profit Graph look like to you? Just immediate answer that comes to your head without thinking about it.

  o Yeah, that's interesting. I mean, I guess, if she does step in ... All I see is this one lump sum, but that's not true ... It would actually, it would be more, it would multiply.

- Are there any gaps in this graph? Does it start immediately?

  o I don't see a graph.

- It's missing.

  o I see something, but it's not a graph.

- Then she's not there.

  o I don't think that she ... I feel very shut-down energy from her.

- Okay, then this is currently not an ideal client for your business. That information could save you a lot of time trying to sell them and following up to no end result.

  o Great!

- Pick someone else - an existing client you have. What do you see for that Profit Graph?

  o That, I actually can connect with a lot more. It's interesting because I don't think that I actually think in Profit Graph per client. The way that I'm visually getting it is actually that it's more of this almost like a multiplication and expansion is what it feels like. It's actually that yes, there's this one person and then she will continue to ... It's almost like a feeding and a blooming as she refers other people to me and keeps working with me and keeps buying things that I'm offering, and things like that.

The other graph I usually look at when selling is the Joy Graph. You can look at graphs for any aspect that is important to you. For me, profit and joy in my clients is key,

How much joy is this client going to bring me, because I don't want to work with clients who are a pain in the ass to deal with, draining my joy even if they bring me lots of profits.

Just like the way you analyze the Profit Graph, you can look at the Joy Graph. Are there gaps in it? Does it go up and down? Is it on the up? Does it end after a certain period of time? You can tell a lot of information from this to decide if you want to work on selling them and what to expect in the business relationship.

When visualizing future graphs, you just take the first thing that comes to your mind. You're not trying to calculate the graphs. You're not sitting down and doing sums. You're just saying, "What's my first thought that comes to mind?" That's true for all intuition things. It's always the first call, never go to second-guess because the second-guesses come from your ego mind.

If you are concerned that you tend to be a negative person, then I recommend before you visualize graphs that you TLC (To the Light Connect - see Chapter 1 for more details). Once you connect to the light, you're going to have positive thinking and more accurate graphs.

Intuitive Sales Meetings

There is a saying that I learned in Sandler Sales training that I have found to be true over years of selling.

"All things being equal, people buy from people that they like.

All things not being equal, people buy from people they like."

In traditional sales, you may use various techniques to get a prospect to like you so that they are more likely to buy from you:

- Match and mirror their tone of voice, speed of speaking and body language

- Mention their name a few times in the conversation

- Listen more than you talk

- Ask questions to project understanding the prospect

These are all good and you can go much further and faster by using your intuitive skills, too.

First, as always, TLC. Then ask:

- WWIT for _____ (your prospect's name) to like me?

- WWIT for ____ to trust me?

Take any inspired actions that you get for this particular person and situation.

There are some more advanced business intuition methods you can apply: Meeting Magic and Heart Connection Meetings. Whether you are meeting in person, on the phone or via email, intuition can help you connect better with your prospect. (Yes, I consider emailing to be a "meeting" that these skills can be applied to. And as much modern selling starts in email, this is an important skill to master.) Let's look at those in the next section.

Meeting Magic

Here is how to do Meeting Magic:

- It can be for a physical meeting, phone call, single email or, in your case, bulk email.

- Get into your heart space (can visualize a loving scene or imagine an elevator going down from your head to your heart)

- Imagine a room where you will meet the other people. In your case or phone calls, this is purely imaginary

- Ground each corner and put a rose in each corner to clear the space

- Put a rose at the door to the room so that only people who will fit the intent you put in below can enter. In your case, only those people will see and open the email

- Bow to all the people entering to greet them

- Put some words into the room for your intent, e.g., "joy, profits, success"

That is all there is to it.

I usually do the visualization for about a minute. You can ask your intuition how long to do on a particular day. You also may feel the energy shift when it is "done."

(I learned Meeting Magic from the book "<u>What Do You Mean the Third Dimension Is Going Away?</u>" by Jim Self. It is on page 175. There are many other useful energy work methods in the book. I have been using it with good results since 2013.)

When I used Meeting Magic for my 6,000 email list using my third eye to do the psychic work, as most people do when visualizing, I sometimes get a headache. If you get this, then you can also do psychic work from other chakras such as your root, or off your body entirely. Or just ask your angels to do the Meeting Magic for you instead.

In addition, you can visualize gold threads connecting you, your company and people via your email offer and draw them in like you were fishing. Similar to the Star Field method in the section above.

If you want to play with this more, you could do a split test by doing Meeting Magic on people whose email start with a-m and not on those who start n-z. Then compare results.

Heart Connection Meetings

Heart connection sales is a method that can boost your sales closing rate and make sales meetings easier, too. Here is how to do it:

- TLC (To the Light, Connect - see Chapter 1 for details on how to do this.)

- TLC your prospect by sending light from above and below them into them.

- Visualize light connecting your heart to their heart.

I do this when meeting with prospects, and I notice that then it matters less the words that I say and we still get to a sale. I also feel calmer than when I don't connect to the light, which helps the sale, too.

When I say "meeting," this could be in person, on GoToMeeting, on the phone, sending connect requests in LinkedIn, messaging in Facebook, Tweeting or in email.

In the case of email or LinkedIn, I do the heart connection process when I send the message and see it happening when my prospect reads the message in the future, too. From the point of view of your intuition, there is no linear time anyway – it is all one moment.

If multiple people are in the meeting, I see all the hearts being connected with light. I maintain this during the whole meeting as much as I can. For example, with 3 people, I visualize a triangle of light lines connecting everyone.

Reading Their Budget

Many times in sales, you want to know the prospect's budget, but they are reluctant to give an indication of how much they have to spend. Too many I expect.

You can find out budgets by asking your intuition!

That way you don't spend days writing a proposal for their project that costs $100k only to discover that they only want to spend $10k.

Ask your intuition: "What is this person going to be happy spending?"

I did a project recently and my intuition said, "They could spend $110k on this project." And I chose to bid it for $69k., That was the number that my intuition said to bid it at, but I knew they would have paid more. And they were happy! And they signed immediately. And they have money available for add-on items later.

I got this budget information without lots of emails or meetings. I felt what energy they had. I had talked to them about the project scope, but we hadn't discussed price or budget at all.

Keep a journal of what your intuition says about prospects' budgets and see how successful it is looking back on it.

If the number you get from your intuition isn't good for your profitability, then either take it as a No or you can send light into it and the prospect to clear the issue they have around budget. See if you can get the number to increase. Sometimes you can shift it, sometimes not, in which case, you are clear that this prospect is not going to work out.

For example, if your intuition tells you "Hey, they don't even want to pay $500" and you know it's going to cost at least $10k ... You can just say very matter of factly, "Hey, I'm just getting this impression that you don't really have a $10k budget here. Is that right?" You don't have to be mean or anything. And they might say "Whoa, no, I can't do 10k."

That is a win! You just saved yourself hours of time writing a proposal and holding meetings for a sale that was lost to start with.

It also acts as a negative reverse. That is, where in sales you back away from the prospect energetically.

It's a bit like a pendulum. If you try and push them, "You need this. Buy it from me!" They're like, "Whoa." Back away.

But if you pull away from them by saying "I'm not sure if this is going to be a fit." Then they will try and come back to you saying something to the effect of "Yes, yes! Let us buy from you! Please!"

On a practical 3D level, I'm totally fine asking people their budget. You just say, "Look. We do websites and we can either do the Ford Taurus website or we could do the Cadillac website, or we could do the Rolls Royce website. And those would typically cost $10-20k, $40-60k, or $150-250k. Where do you feel you are?" That's a way to do it in traditional sales.

Sales Scale with WWIT

A common sales technique is to ask the prospect to rate something on a 0-10 scale, where 0 = it sucks and 10 = it is wonderful. Like this:

- How do you feel about buying from my company right now on a scale of 0-10? (any number is ok with me)

- How do you feel about your current system on a scale of 0-10?

- No one is perfect. How do you feel about your current vendor on a scale of 0-10?

The number they give provides some useful feedback, but the gold in this method is the next question you ask. (After you nurture them by thanking them for sharing that number, of course).

- WWIT (What Would It Take) to get that to a 10?

Then shut up for as long as it takes for them to speak and explain what it would take. Their answer will tell you exactly what you need to do to make the sale, or how their current system or vendor could be improved, which is your opportunity to open the door to a trial purchase from your company!

After the Sale

So you have made the sale. What about customer care? Yes, that is another part of the sales process.

A lot of businesses hire staff to do customer care or tech support, and they make a complete balls-up of it because they're following rules rather than responding to the person and using their intuition.

This is an example that I experienced personally. I've used both Hootsuite and Buffer for social media post scheduling. Hootsuite, technically, does pretty much what you need, but their customer service reps were not helpful. It seemed like they were following their little SOP (Standard Operating Procedure), and they're doing what they're supposed to do, but they don't actually solve your problem.

The ones at Buffer may or may not solve your problem, but they're very personable, and they've heard your pain, and I am left with the feeling that they're going to deal with it. And they follow up to make sure the fix worked.

It was a much better experience.

This is something that a lot of companies get wrong. They think that the high-touch interaction with the customer ends for them once the sale is closed whereas it's really an ongoing relationship. Even if you sell products or one-time services rather than recurring services, you want them to order again. Or to recommend you to somebody else. Or write nice things about you on social media.

This brings you and your customers more joy and increases the average Lifetime Value (LTV) of your customers.

Firing Clients

Not every client qualifies to be your client. Not every prospect caught is good enough to be a client for your business. They may not satisfy your ideal client criteria.

I recommend you regularly fire clients from your business, the ones who are a poor fit for you.

I used to do a spreadsheet for this doing the process logically. It took quite a lot of time. I would rank them on a 1-5 scale on questions such as:

- Do they pay on time?

- Are they joyful to work with?

- Do they give me referrals?

Then I'd give them a score and the bottom ones I would fire. By firing a client, I mean I would have a conversation saying our company had changed focus and we are no longer a fit for them and I'd give them a referral to someone else who wanted the business. "It is not you, it is me."

Instead you can ask your intuition which clients are the bright and shiny ones and which ones seem dull.

Whichever way you evaluate and fire poor-fit clients, you will feel better afterwards. And when I've done this, I got new and better clients really quickly.

Case Study: Marcelle Bottini's Intuitive Team Story

Marcelle Bottini owns a school in Rio, Brazil that she founded 6 years ago. It has a large team and clients such as oil companies and TV stations. She told me in an interview:

> "Even though I had developed my school using intuition and meditation from the beginning, now that the school is already developed and with a big team and huge clients, I started to forget about these abilities. Learning these intuition tools brought this back to me. With practical exercises I could focus on every aspect of my company, learning to manage it using energy.
>
> After 6 years as an established company, it has been new to me to work and manage the team remotely. The workshop helped me

manage them successfully online. Including helping make a sale. The team was very tense.

We had the opportunity of a contract with a big oil and gas company and it was the first time that they would have to do the sales presentation without me and in English, a second language for them. I improved their confidence by the TLC and WWIT tools. I had spiritual encounters with the prospect - I could intuit what was important to them and their main objectives so we could build the right presentation for them. After one week, the team went to the presentation and the client already wanted to hire us before they opened their mouths!

And the result was having the team successfully doing their first business sales presentation without me. I used the intuition tools to reinforce the team, teach them to use and trust their own intuition, and as a result we had a new contract with a huge oil and gas company. And this is only the beginning. I'm starting to communicate with my team using these new tools on a regular basis."

Intuitive Deal Making

Making a deal is just another sale, admittedly a larger one and probably with more players. Whether it is a deal to buy another company, to sell your company, to set up a joint-venture, to sell stock or bonds for your company, at the end of the day, it is still a sale.

Use the intuition tools in this chapter to make the sale go easier and be more profitable and joyful for you. (If you don't do deals, this section also provides a concise summary of the tools in this chapter).

Usually in a business sale, it's a one-time deal where you never see the buyer again. You will probably be involved with them for years - in initial negotiations and then an earn out period. So you want to check "Is there a good relationship here?" over the long term. Even if the sales price seems good, it still might not be a good joy fit if they are hard to work with over time.

In particular notice how your body responds. Your gut or other body parts may be giving you information about the other party that you mind does not know yet.

For example, in 1961, Ray Kroc's intuition told him to go ahead on the deal to buy out the McDonald brothers' small burger business with a $2.7 million loan.... against his lawyers' rational advice. As of today it is worth $99,000 million. Quite a return on investment.

Define Your Ideal Partner

Even if the deal opportunity has come up before you had a chance to do this, take a moment to step back, TLC (To the Light, Connect), separate your energy from others (using cord cutting or other methods) and writing down what an ideal partner for this type of deal is for you. Then compare to this potential partner. If there are major items that are a bad fit or you have missing information on certain characteristics, then you know to either kill the deal or find more information.

Ask WWIT

WWIT (What Would It Take) to reach an ideal deal with this partner or someone better? Adding in the "someone better" allows your intuition to suggest even better ideas that you may not have considered.

Find Ideal Partners Using Intuition

If you have several possible partners, then you can use Joy and Profit Graphs to compare them. In particular, look to see if the graph has breaks in it or ends earlier than you expect as those are signs of a negotiation that feels like a struggle or a failed one.

If you have a long list of suspects, feel which one in the list is "sticky" and follow up on that one.

If you don't have any potential partners in mind, then the Abundance Tree or Starfield visualizations can help attract them.

You can add light to your proposal or deal one pager by adding light TLCing it (adding light to it from above and below).

Reading Pricing and Fit

You can use your intuition to read what pricing and terms will be a good fit for a particular potential partner. One way to do this is to use the Two Chairs Method from this chapter.

You may also get intuitive information on how they feel about you in the deal, their deal-making approach or some red flags that are useful to know in the negotiation.

Successful Deal Meetings

You can use Meeting Magic and the Heart Connection Meetings tool from this chapter to make meetings go well. In the case of Heart Connection, you will be connecting with all the people in the meeting, not just one on one as you might do in a smaller sales meeting.

Removing Negative Energy From the Deal

If you notice negative energy in the other company, (or even in your team), about the deal, you can use the Energy Vampire clearing methods from Chapter 7, Intuitive Teams to shift it so the deal can implement successfully.

Homeplay

- Get clear in writing on who your ideal client is

- Ask yourself: WWIT to find them?

- Play with feeling lists of prospects, then compare your intuition with your results from contacting them

- Play with the Abundance Tree or Star Field visualization

- Evaluate current hot prospects with Profit/Joy Graphs or the Two Chairs Method

- Try out Meeting Magic on your next meeting

- Combine traditional and intuitive sales methods if you are new to intuition and just want an extra edge in your sales.

Bonus Materials

The bonus materials from this chapter are at www.intuitiveleadershipmastery.com/bonus/

- Sample client avatars (doc)

- Abundance Tree visualization (audio)

CHAPTER 6

Intuitive Marketing

"In this ever-changing society, the most powerful and enduring brands are built from the heart. They are real and sustainable. Their foundations are stronger because they are built with the strength of the human spirit, not an ad campaign. The companies that are lasting are those that are authentic." – *Howard Schultz, CEO of Starbucks*

Traditional Marketing

In traditional marketing you don't know which actions will attract your next client or when. You advertise to a lot of people, a certain percentage show interest and become prospects (and then, hopefully, eventually buy from you).

You may have a marketing funnel where members of your ideal audience enter and at each stage, you believe that they are showing more and more interest in buying.

For example:

- You might have lots of content written for your website in the hope that it will engage potential buyers (this is content marketing).

- You might spend a lot of time and money writing stories and talking with journalists and bloggers to get them to cover your product or service (this is PR, or public relations).

- You might go to networking events or spend time on social media in order to connect with prospects (this is network or social marketing).

It is a logical approach to the uncertainty of knowing ahead of time who is interested in buying from your business. As a marketing pioneer, John Wanamaker said:

> *"Half the money I spend on advertising is wasted; the trouble is I don't know which half."*

What if you could know ahead of time which ads will bring more profits or joy to you?

Intuition gives you a more efficient way by helping you to define and attract your ideal prospects faster than traditional marketing. You can either use these methods together with traditional ones such as direct email and advertising, or you can use them stand-alone.

Clarify Your Ideal Prospect

Just as in the sales chapter, it's key to be clear about who you are focusing your marketing efforts on. Before you can successfully attract prospects, you must define who your ideal prospect is. Both demographic (age, gender, geography, etc.) and what they are like as people. Their personality, their hopes, desires and pains — especially as their "pains or gains" relate to your product or service.

Create an avatar — an imaginary ideal prospect. Write a backstory about them, add a photo, write about what they do in their life, write about the emotions they feel when they have the pain or gain that you solve.

Two Chair Method

Imagine two chairs facing either other. You are sitting in one chair and your ideal prospect in the other chair (see Chapter 3, Hiring, for more detailed instructions). Then notice:

- Is your ideal prospect looking at you or are they distracted? If the latter, then WWIT to get their attention, and keep it?

- Do they have feet in your vision? If not, WWIT to ground them?

- Anything else you notice about them? What does that mean to you?

B2C vs B2B vs B2G

In B2C (Business To Consumer marketing) you are selling to an individual for their personal use, or at most to a family for family use. Usually one person or at most two people (husband and wife) will be your ideal prospect in that situation.

With B2B (Business To Business) or B2G (Business To Government), you will still have your initial ideal prospect, but there may be other decision-makers, influencers or a whole buying committee involved. You may need several avatars to represent the different interests involved. You will need to both work with each one separately and as a group. For the group intuitive marketing, I use Meeting Magic (see below for details on this).

You also create an ideal company prospect profile. Then have your company sit in the first chair and your ideal company in the other one. Then ask yourself the same questions as with individuals:

- Is your ideal prospect looking at you or are they distracted? If the latter, then WWIT to get their attention, and keep it?

- Do they have feet in your vision? If not, WWIT to ground them?

- Anything else you notice about them? What does that mean to you?

Attracting Your Ideal Prospect

In all cases, asking a powerful WWIT question will help attract your ideal prospects to you:

- WWIT to attract my ideal prospect to me?

- See what inspired actions come to you.

In the case of B2B or B2G, you will repeat this for each avatar that you created. And ask it for your company profile:

- WWIT to attract my ideal company prospect to me?

As is the case with all uses of What Would It Take (WWIT), it helps to 'To The Light, Connect' (TLC) first. It's also important to be patient: you may need to ask the question many times to get full answers from your intuition.

If you get an answer that you don't know how to immediately action, then keep asking Nested WWITs until you get to a step that you can take action on today.

For example:

- WWIT to attract my ideal company prospect to me?
  - Have better branding
  - WWIT to have better branding?
    - Ask my friend Ali for ideas
    - Ask my new marketing manager for ideas

Branding As Energy and Attraction

Branding is more than logo, graphics, color schemes, taglines and fonts. It is the energy that your company gives off to prospects. As well as improving your physical branding, fliers and websites, you can improve their energy. You can make them more attractive to prospects. You can shift how they feel when they see them. Here is how.

Decide what intent you have for your branding. For example, "Our branding inspires prospects with confidence, joy and connection with us."

Then ask: WWIT to bring this intent to life? Clear any blocks by TLCing them with light from above and below . For example:

- WWIT to have our branding inspire our ideal prospects with confidence, joy and connection with us?

- Say, "Everywhere that is blocked, release, relight across all realities," while you visualize light coming from above and below into the block.

Ads, Landing Pages and Meeting Magic

You can make your ads and website landing pages more effective by adding energetic intent to them. As above, decide what energy you want prospects to feel when they see your ad or view your landing page, then ask yourself what action you want them to take, and design the assets accordingly.

For example, for an ad, use a WWIT to add that energy to it:

- WWIT for prospects to feel excited, trust us and click on our ads?

- WWIT for prospects to feel connected to us and joyful and click on the Opt-in button on this landing page?

You can also do Meeting Magic. See Chapter 5, Sales, for details on doing this. You would use the same characteristics you listed above in setting up the "meeting" with your prospects viewing your ad or landing page.

- TLC.

- Imagine a room where you will meet the other people. In the case of an ad, this is purely imaginary.

- Ground each corner and put a rose in each corner to clear the space.

- Put another rose at the door to the room so that only people who will fit the intent you put in below can enter. In this, only those people will see your ad.

- Bow to all the people entering the room to greet them.

- Put some words into the room for your intent, e.g., "joy, profits, success."

You can do the same technique when sending out email campaigns or direct mail to thousands of people.

One CEO used this before a presentation they were doing and afterward told me:

> "Amazing stuff! Did it today right before my workshop and yes, the audience is warm, open and engaging!!! Exactly as envisioned."

Youngest Age Pattern Recycling tool

When you notice a pattern of behavior in your business that you want to change, or when you just feel lower emotions on the Hawkins scale such as guilt or shame, you can use the following tool to clear the issue and negative feelings. You can also use it to permanently clear the root causes of the problem.

Here are the questions to ask yourself:

- How do you feel when this thing in your business is happening? (What emotions and body sensations do you feel, not thoughts.)

- What is the youngest age you felt the same way? (You don't have to have a conscious memory of the age - just say the first age that comes into your mind)

- Who was this with? (again, just go with the first person that comes to you. Perhaps your mom, dad, a teacher, a child or other)

- TLC (To the Light, Connect) yourself

- TLC your younger self who first had this same set of emotions and body sensations by visualizing light coming from above and below them into their body. And TLC the pattern that you are clearing by visualizing it as a shape in front of you that you send light into from above and below.

We look at a practical example of using this tool to increase revenue in the next section.

Case Study: Gabby's 10 Minutes To A 10% Revenue Increase

Gabby Wallace was stuck in her business. She is CEO of <u>Go Natural English</u> that has a YouTube channel with millions of views, but she was getting drained by the people writing weird comments on her videos.

This was important because she makes hundreds of videos a year to promote her business. These comments meant she was resisting making new videos, which is a problem since she is the face of her business (as many CEOs are). This is a common issue when you become famous in your field — self-sabotage comes up. This means that you take two steps forward on a goal and then one step back, (or sometimes ten steps back!).

It was getting to the point where a business friend told her "Hey, your videos really aren't quite as sparkly as they used to be." She dreaded getting on the camera anymore.

So I did a clearing with her using the Youngest Age Pattern Recycle tool (see prior section above) that fixed this issue in 10 minutes and let her add 10% to her annual revenue.

The first question was:

- How do you feel when this thing in your business is happening? (What emotions and body sensations do you feel, not thoughts.)

She felt abandoned and discouraged.

The second question was:

- What is the youngest age you felt the same way? (You don't have to have a conscious memory of the age, just say the first age that comes into your mind.)

For Gabby, the youngest age she recalled feeling the same way was at 3 years old, with her father. When he didn't pay attention to her, she felt abandoned and discouraged.

She had been recreating this pattern throughout her childhood, school, early jobs and now in her business.

We cleared the pattern in a few minutes by sending light to her younger self, visualizing the pattern that she created then and seeing light clear it from above and below.

After a few minutes of this, the issue felt clear. She then asked herself:

- WWIT (What Would It Take) to take my business to the next level?

She got an immediate inspired action (a new business idea) which adds 10% to her annual revenue, and now finds it easy to create new videos and is not bothered by viewer comments.

Often you are the main person getting in the way of greater business success. The only thing that's stopping your business getting to where you want to go is yourself and the patterns you are carrying with you from childhood. We often carry crap — limiting beliefs and unhealed trauma that we have from childhood. We reenact it in our business.

Business, in many ways, is a spiritual growth pursuit. In this way, it is like marriage.

Perhaps you have been in a relationship or marriage, and although it might have been challenging, you came out of it growing spiritually. The same thing can happen in business. Problems come up and if you deal with the roots of the issue, you will grow spiritually.

In my opinion, that's the spiritual reason behind all the millions of driven CEOs and other business leaders who have incarnated on this planet. Yes, we make money, we create cool stuff, we have fun. But it's also so we can be better human beings and we can grow spiritually.

Case Study: Mandi Uses WWIT To Get Referrals

Mandi Ellefson, CEO of the Hands Off CEO, was thanked by an influential person in her field. So she asked her intuition: WWIT (What Would It Take) to know what to ask of him? Intuition told her to ask for an endorsement. (My brain's idea was something entirely different that wouldn't have worked as well — trust your own intuition!) Here is what he said after she asked him:

> *"I'm a big fan of Mandi's, so much so that we include her training and require our clients to go through it as part of our programs. Recently we had Mandi speak to a large group of our best clients, and there's just no doubt... she is a true expert in scaling your business and your freedom. She shared high-value content, was very engaging with the group, and made it relevant and actionable. Our clients consistently tell me how critical Mandi's training and content has been to their success. I'm grateful to have her in my corner!!"*

Wow! That is a powerful endorsement, and exactly what she needed to build her speaking resume and have more credibility on her website. This guy will be twice as big in a year, too.

She told me that *"The big deal here is I have had no idea how to leverage all the many amazing connections I have. It's actually opening up my eyes to the possibilities now just thinking about it. WWIT... to know the right way to help a partner... how to best leverage a relationship to be win-win, and which calls are worth doing."*

Homeplay

- Clarify who your ideal prospect is with a bullet point list

- Play with using WWIT to attract them and take an inspired action that comes to you

- Try out Meeting Magic on one of your marketing methods and notice what occurs

- The next time you notice a self-sabotaging pattern in your business or just feel lower vibration emotions, experiment with the Youngest Age Pattern Recycling tool

Bonus Materials

The bonus materials from this chapter are at
www.intuitiveleadershipmastery.com/bonus/

- Gabby healing with Youngest Age Pattern Recycle tool (audio)

CHAPTER 7

Intuitive Teams

"People work better when they know what the goal is and why. It is important that people look forward to coming to work in the morning and enjoy working." - *Elon Musk, CEO of Tesla Motors and SpaceX*

S ome teams in a company sync well together and create wonderful work. Others are a cesspit of drama, office politics and that create negative work. By negative work I mean they not only do not produce anything useful for the business, but they take up time and energy from other teams that are productive.

With the intuition tools in this chapter, you can consciously create and maintain teams that work well together and are productive. You can discover hidden issues in your teams before they manifest as problems and fix them energetically without stress and lost time.

The most important things you can help team members to learn is to TLC (To the Light, Connect) and the WWIT tool (What Would It Take).

You can pick future team members who are more intuitive by adding this skill to your ideal candidate profile and use the tools from Chapter 3 (Hiring).

Energy Vampires

You want your teams to work well together towards their company goals, but "energy vampires" in your teams can destroy teamwork and lower energy.

An energy vampire is a person that just sucks the life out of you. They're draining and often depressing to be around. Perhaps you have experienced someone like that already in one of your teams, or in your personal life.

If it's someone in your team, you could just fire them, since they're not currently a good culture fit, or you could give them a disciplinary review and hope that they improve their behaviour.

Those are the traditional ways to deal with problem employees, but this problem goes beyond one or two difficult people. If you don't fix the energy pattern *in you* that attracted this kind of person to your business, the situation is likely to repeat again until you learn the spiritual lesson from it. The tools in this chapter help you do that.

To clear energy vampires from your business, you can cut cords with them (see the chapter on the Intuition Toolkit for details on how to do this). The energetic cord that connects them to you is how they suck your energy and drain the joy and productivity from your business.

Alternatively, you could TLC them — send lots of light into them from above and below.

Business dynamics are often similar to family dynamics. When you hire someone into the business, they may see you as an authority figure and treat you like their mother or father. As a result, all of the patterns they have in relating to their parents tend to get re-enacted with you. For example, they may be always asking you for permission to do tasks, or might show up late to meetings or talk back to you when you lay out your expectations of them.

Ideally, you won't hire people who will bring this kind of baggage with them and who won't have any major family issues. We talked about how to do that by writing down your ideal candidate in the chapter on Hiring, and I strongly suggest you review that material if you're dealing with a difficult employee at the moment, to see where the hiring process might have gone wrong and to unravel how you can do things differently next time.

But if you've already got an energy vampire in a valuable role, then I suggest you might work on clearing them. Send them light, cut all the cords you can find, or ask "WWIT for this person to become an energy giver and a valuable source of positivity and productivity for our team?"

As well as sending light to individuals on your team, you can also send light to the team as a whole. Visualise each person being connected to every other person with lines of light, connecting all their hearts together. Then add your intentions for your team to the visualization. For example, it might be your intention that they work easily and well together, and that they make a specific part of the business grow in an effective way.

Handling energy vampires is one of the most important things you can do to make your business more joyful and effective. That negative draining needs to be removed from your team, so either fire them or upgrade them.

Typically what I do with an energy vampire in a valuable role is a serious upgrade to their energy. If they are draining me or causing me problems, I send them so much light they're either going to improve dramatically and have a radical change, or they're going to get absolutely sick of it all and leave my business.

You create the reality you want. If a team member or outside contractor is not playing ball, then it's on you to change the situation. Once I was having trouble with a cell phone company in Singapore. *I upgraded the whole company* because they were getting in the way of progress.

After this spiritual upgrade, the company did an about-face and gave me what I wanted. It's always the same with team members, too — they either get on board or get out. It sounds like tough love, and it is, but remember that this is *your* business, *your* vision, and if they're going to be in your reality, they'd better be ready for it.

Reading Team Energy

The energy of your team as a whole affects what results the team can create for your business. The collective energy also affects your personal energy and the energy of each individual team member.

Think of a team as a complete, separate being, rather than being composed of individuals. Ask your intuition what the team's vibration is. Is the overall sense of their energy shame, fear, pride, love? See the list of energy levels in Chapter One and use your intuition to work out which level the team is on today.

Then you can ask WWIT (What Would It Take) to get the team's energy to the next level? What inspired actions come to you? Ideally you want your teams to be at level 500 (love) or higher because then they will achieve their goals more easily.

You can also set energetic intentions into your teams, either using WWIT, Meeting Magic (discussed in the chapter on Marketing) or another intuition tool of your choosing. Here is how to use WWIT for this:

Exercise: Start by TLC (To the Light, Connect) each team member. Then TLC the team energy as a whole. Get clarity on what intentions you have for the team, for example, that the team communicates really well, is profitable and joyful, and reaches goals A, B and C this month. Then ask a WWIT to achieve that:

- WWIT for this team to communicate really well?

- WWIT for this team to be profitable and joyful?

- WWIT for this team to reach goals A, B and C this month?

Then see what inspired actions you get. Make sure you record anything that comes to you so you can roll it out with the team in the future.

You can also have all the team members ask the same question in a team meeting. I recommend you have each person TLC before they ask the WWIT question so that they get better quality answers.

As well as reading and increasing the team's energy, you can also use other intuitive leadership tools on the team as a whole. For example, check for any energy cords draining the team's energy and cut them away. Or look for any other energy drains on the team and clear them so that nothing gets in the way of the team and its goals.

Team Chairs Methods

We have used the Two Chairs Method to read intuitive information on one person (see Chapter 5 for details). There are two ways you can extend this to team information reading.

Firstly, you can put the collective team being in the other chair in order to read information about the team. Is it looking at you? What does its head look like? Does it have legs and feet? What color is it?

For example, if you see that the team being is looking in many directions at once with its head flickering around in multiple directions, that might indicate that the team is not focused in one direction and is not looking at you. To fix this, use WWIT and send light to the team being. WWIT for it to be focused on its goals?

Secondly, you can visualize all the individual team members, and you, sitting on chairs in a circle. Then visualize a copy of you, standing as an observer outside the circle to notice how each team member appears and where they are looking during this process.

You might notice that some team members are larger than others. Some might be shining out more bright light than others, some might be more grounded than others. To change this and balance out the energy amongst the team members, you can shine light into the appropriate parts of their bodies. For example, if one team member is contracted and bent over, add light from above and below, and visualize them sitting up straight, bringing their confidence and abilities into the mix. If a team member has no legs, then add more light from below to ground them and help them to be more focused and connected to the team's goals.

If you want all the team members to focus on the common goals you have set out for them, then imagine that the goals are in the middle of the circle and that you are adding light to them. Have everyone look at the common goals, then see them happy and smiling as they achieve these goals with ease.

You might also want them to pay more attention to you. In this case, shine light from the standing observer copy of you to each other member of the team. Connect your heart to each of their hearts and shine light to their eyes so it's easier for them to pay attention to you.

You can use the Joy and Profit Graph intuition tools to predict how a team will perform over the next few months or years. See Chapter 5 (Sales) for more details on this graphs method.

You can either look at your personal joy level in the Joy Graph or the joy level of the team as a whole. If you are emotionally connected to the team, these will be similar. If you are separated from the team, then they may be different.

For example, looking at the team's Joy Graph, you may see it starting low then increasing over time, or perhaps it ends after 18 months which might indicate that the team ceases to exist then.

If you don't like how the graph looks, you can send light to the parts of the graph you want to change and ask yourself, "WWIT (What Would It Take) for it to be the way I want it to be?"

You can similarly work on the Profit Graph for a team.

Creating A Safe Space for Your Team

Teams work better, have more joy and create more profits when they are in a safe space. A space allows for them to express their ideas and to experiment with new methods for working better.

When team members are empowered and feel engaged with the team goals, results happen faster. Part of that is sharing team goals explicitly with the team and keeping the goals front of mind at all times.

Good ways to do this include...

- Write the goals on a whiteboard in the team meeting space

- Have all team members co-create a vision board for the goals and put in the team room so they see it every day

- Share team goal KPIs (Key Performance Indicator numbers) with all team members every week. Include a traffic light color for each KPI (green = good, yellow = needs improvement, red = stop everything and fix this issue now)

Clearly sharing your company's vision, brand vision and team mission all help a company to operate at a more profitable and joyful level. We look more at creating Vision for your team or company in Chapter 8 (Visioning).

Co-Creating and Empowering Your Teams

Co-creating a team project helps team members to be more engaged with the company, the mission of the team and with each other. Co-creating means that each person on the team has a say in how the goals are reached and can implement improved ways of getting there.

If you are a leader who is afraid to give up control, this might be hard at first. Perhaps you are used to telling everyone what to do and how to do it, but if you want your team to function at a higher level, this is a very important barrier to break past.

It is not that the team members can do whatever they want. When starting out, you can set limits on what input you want and how the final decision will be made.

This method takes more time up-front than the traditional authoritarian approach of telling people what to do, but it saves time over the course of the project because empowered team members know what to do without having to be told exactly what to do in every possible scenario. They will come up with on-the-spot fixes for project roadblocks rather than wasting time waiting to get direction from you.

This saves a lot of time for you and reduces your stress. Perhaps more importantly, it saves team member time and reduces their stress, too. Finally, it makes each project more efficient and profitable, because resources are not being wasted on micromanaging every aspect.

Think of co-created projects as an investment in the team and its goals. It helps to create a strong team that can get results without your constantly having to babysit them. In a strong team, the whole is greater than the sum of its parts, and the team will come up with amazing solutions to reach its goals... and have fun doing it.

The Agile movement in software development and now in other functional areas is a common way that companies co-create in teams. The team leader (or "scrum master" in Agile speak) is there to keep the team on focus and to empower team members, rather than to tell them how to do their jobs.

The Lockheed Skunk Works was an early example of this kind of team. In July 1938 they were given a difficult goal, were kept away from the authoritarian management methods of the rest of the company and were given freedom to come up with their own solutions. The small group of engineers in the Skunk Works made the first prototype of the P-38 Lightning fighter aircraft. They worked in a separate room and other employees were kept away. The team secretly added advanced features to the aircraft such as the then-novel flush-riveted aluminum body that allowed it to be the first 400 mph fighter plane in the world. The team, given autonomy and trust like this, changed the way the aviation industry looked at the possibilities of engineering.

Another good example is the large Semco corporation of Brazil. The book "Maverick: The Success Story Behind the World's Most Unusual Workplace" by CEO Ricardo Semler gives the details and story of how Semco co-creates its products. The book shows how the company overcame constant strikes, crazy inflation and outdated products to become one of the most successful and innovative companies in Brazil (or the world, for that matter).

Empowering Team Members with WWIT

When I lead a team, I ask each team member to report once a week with a list of:

- Upcoming challenges for future tasks

- What they plan to do in the coming week

- What they have done in the past week

Then I can encourage them to use WWITs (What Would It Take) on the challenges to come up with solutions or to identify where they need to ask for help.

Asking team members "WWIT to reach our project goal(s)?" is a good way to get team engagement and input. It focuses them on solutions rather than stressing out over problems or arguing amongst themselves.

Empowering your teams via co-creation, TLC and WWIT has an enormous improvement on team energy, results and joy. It also lets people grow more personally and in their careers. It reduces burnout, which lowers the rate of people quitting and needing to be replaced. (This is important — as we saw in the chapter on hiring, staff churn is very expensive for both your company and team morale.)

If an individual doesn't feel empowered in their workplace, it disempowers the whole team. A work group is like a machine — if you have just one broken piece, then it affects the whole machine's performance.

If one team member isn't aligned with the company's goals, or is an energy vampire, then it disempowers the whole team and can derail the progress you want to see for each of the goals you've set.

Another way to access your intuition around your team dynamic is to ask your intuition about the project or team beings and their desires. Ask:

- What does the project want?
- What does the team want?

Instead of the team creating the project results, consider that the project itself is a spiritual being and is utilizing your company and team members to create itself. Many authors that I have talked to feel this way about the best books they have written. It was not so much that they wrote the book, but that "the book wrote them."

Homeplay

- How many energy vampires are in your team? Who are they?
- Play with one of the energy clearing methods for energy vampires: cord cutting, TLC or upgrading.
- Write down one way that you allow energy vampires in your team.
- Play with the multiple chairs method to read team energy and to shift it.

- Play with team Joy and Profit Graphs. What did you learn from this?

- Ask at team meetings: "WWIT to reach our project goal?"

- WWIT to empower your team members?

- What project could you give your team to practice co-creating?

Bonus Materials

The bonus materials from this chapter are at
www.intuitiveleadershipmastery.com/bonus/

- Interview with Nicole Seelinger about teams and co-creation (audio)

CHAPTER 8

Intuitive Visioning

"Intuition will tell the thinking mind where to look next." - *Jonas Salk, Inventor of the Polio vaccine*

The Traditional Approach to Visioning

T raditionally, visioning is something that happens at the start of each year. You sit down and think about what you want for the year ahead. Then from that, you extrapolate annual goals for your business or department, and finally dictate them to your staff. If you are lucky, they will be motivated and happy to get on board with what you have envisioned, and will work hard to achieve the goals. More likely, they (and you!) will get distracted over the course of the year by inevitable fire fighting, bright, new "shiny objects" to chase after, and before you know it, all your goals are forgotten.

Then in Q4, there may be a frantic push to reach the goals when it becomes apparent that no one has been working on them consistently. This tends to create a stressful environment for the last few months of the year. It does not empower your teams and produces less results and joy than is possible and sets you up to repeat this ineffective cycle again next year.

Meet You+3

There's a much easier and more effective way to vision your goals for your business. Meet yourself in 3 years' time — AKA you+3. Ask you+3 who they are, what they have done, and the exact step that they took to get there. Below is an exercise you can use to do this.

Exercise:

Close your eyes and place both feet on the ground. TLC (To the Light, Connect - see Chapter 1 for details on how to do this). Visualize yourself in 3 years' time sitting in front of you. Ask yourself the following questions and give the first answer that comes to you. (The first answer is your intuition speaking, your ego comes via second-guessing.) Don't analyze your answers or even think about them. You may find it easier to do this speaking out loud and recording on your phone rather than writing things down.

Here are the questions to ask you+3:

- Who are you?

- What are you doing?

- What business do you have?

- What kind of business is it (in term of qualities /characteristics — e.g., busy, peaceful, easy, etc.)

- What have you achieved? (Money, fame, awards, skills.)

- What has your business achieved? (Profit amounts, products released, recognition, awards, revenue.)

- What is your team like? (Staff, clients and vendors.)

- Where is your business located? What kind of place? What is the energy like for you and your team?

- How did you get there?

- What are the exact steps that your future self took to create all this?

- WWIT (What Would It Take) for me, as I am now, to get where you are with ease and grace?

Key: Stay focused on your future self. When I guide clients through this exercise, they often slip back into the present and all the problems they have in their business right now. If that happens, redirect your attention back to your future self as soon as you notice. If possible, do this exercise with a trusted friend who can redirect you back to your future self when you slip.

Letter From Your Future Self

I invite you to write a letter from your future self to your current self that tells you exactly how she got to where they are from where you are now.

Important: Write this letter in the **past tense**. Say things like "I did A. I invested in B . I hired C. I shifted my business by D." Your future self is writing you as you currently are, back in the past.

This is a powerful trick to get your intuitive mind to believe it has already happened.

It is important because we treat the past as having happened with 100% certainty. If you write this letter in the future tense saying things like: "I will do this. I would do that," then that is filled with the energy of doubt, but what you need is an energy of certainty.

Feel the energy of certainty in the following sentences:

- I might do X

- I will do X

- I am doing X

- I have done X

The feeling you get from each of those statements gradually shifts from uncertainty to complete certainty.

By using the energy of certainty, you make it easier to take the actions necessary to create your future, and it enables you to remove doubts from your plan. You also get your intuition working 100% on your plan in the background.

Here is how to take this vision to the next level. You know from the above exercise who you+3 is, what he/she has done, what he/she has and exactly how he/she got there. Now write a letter from your future self to your present day self saying all this. Especially what you did to get there and what emotions you felt. Paint a vivid picture of the story of how you achieved your goals.

I do this with all my staff every year in January. I have them all think about where they want to be in a year's time in my business, in their department. What do they want to create? How do they want to progress? Then they write down how their future self created it all (in the past tense). They each write this letter to themselves and it's amazing: they come back a year later having done all of this cool stuff, and they've gotten to where they wanted to be without any big stress or confusion.

You may already be writing out goals or affirmations, but try writing with the past tense method. You'll get more results, and you'll get them faster.

When I have used this method, it seems as though my goals just come together magically during the year. Coincidences happen. I meet the right people at the right time. When I look back at the end of the time period at my letter again, it is crazy how accurate it can be.

Example Future-Self Letter

Here is a letter written by Dustin, an American CEO, who wrote this letter late in 2016. He is writing as Dustin+1 — himself one year from now.

Date: December 31, 2017

To Dustin,

Another year has come to a close, and oh my, what a year it was!

You had a great year for 2016, but things went into turbo mode in 2017. Firstly, you pretty much doubled sales in just 12 months, to $400,000. Ha ha... and you never thought it was possible, did you?

*Another really cool goal is that your wife, children **and** Mum (who flew in from the US to visit her grandkids) got to spend two weeks in Bangkok at the business conference along with all TownWeb team members.*

The kids enjoyed spending time in the pool with their grandmother. Your wife loved seeing the sights, eating spicy Thai food, going out for massages almost daily, and, of course, filling her Facebook feed with more selfies than you thought possible.

The TownWeb team admired the direction of the business in the past year and that they could get an all-expenses paid holiday to Thailand.

While you did increase the price of your offering to new customers, it was done with an added value of a better product, improved services and a new line of revenue.

Challenges

It wasn't exactly a walk in the park to continually grow the sales while also growing the team, but luckily you took great advice from guys like Jacob Puhl who have paved the way and who gave great advice.

Improvements

Some of the noteworthy improvements you accomplished were gaining a bit of notoriety within the Dynamite Circle community, by offering a real-life case study with monthly reports of how you set out to accomplish your 2017 goals. DC newbies and other aspiring Digital Nomads line up to work with TownWeb as apprentices in hopes of kick-starting their own careers by working for a business that can help them grow.

Products and Services

You made a couple leaps with the level of products and services you offered in 2017. One area was rolling out 400 new forms to people who were interested in using TownWeb Payments (a new line of revenue). This was a great new addition for a complementary product that all customers could use. It seems to be a nice selling feature to attract the business of new clients.

The rebranding you did to the homepage, to the customer sites (admin and front-end) were quite well received within the municipal industry. It boosted the company's profile in municipal marketplace and allowed TownWeb to receive accolades from the design community for ease of use and open governance.

For TownWeb customers, you enhanced the customer service by providing 24/7 support and wowing the customer base with an amazing level of service.

Regarding the web hosting, all issues related to downtime and unexpected technical issues were solved by switching to a series of new hosting providers with 3rd party management, and by only hiring A Player employees and vendors.

Financially
You ended 2017 with $400,000 in total sales.
Keep on keep'n on!
Best regards,
Dustin (from the Future)

Talk With Your Future Self

During the year, you can talk with you future self any time you want to. You can ask them for advice. One way to hear them is to ask yourself:

- WWFMD - What Would Future Me Do?

I usually refer to my future self as Super-Michael. You can call yours Super-<your name>, or whatever name inspires you and them. Then the question becomes:

- WWSMD - What Would Super-Michael Do?

This question is similar in concept to the questions WWJD (What Would Jesus Do) and WWLD (What Would Love Do). This gives your intuition an opportunity to present you with a solution, and for you to connect with the energy you need to solve this issue.

You can apply similar questions to anyone living, dead, in the future or even fictional people. You can ask this of anyone you admire for a certain energy or skill when you want to know how they would handle an issue that you have.

- What Would Richard Branson Do?
- What Would Jeff Bezos Do?
- What Would Oprah Do?
- What Would Steve Jobs Do?
- What Would Henry Ford Do?

Your future self is probably already helping you now. You may not have realized it was them guiding you and sending you love from the future. You'll often get a sense of clarity about a problem, or a solution will come to you that you instinctively know is the right option.

Vision Board

If you are more visual than wordy, you can make a vision board of what you are creating in your business in the future. Take what you learned from your future self and cut out photos and large text from old magazines. Glue them on a piece of poster board, then put it somewhere that you will see it every day.

You can take a photo and make it the background for your phone or computer. Have that image somewhere you will see it every day and can be focused and inspired by it. When you notice yourself looking at your vision board, cultivate a feeling of gratitude for the future that you are creating.

If you are kinesthetic, then you might create a dance or set of movements that symbolize your vision.

Other people create a sigil from the initial letters of their goal. That is a symbol made of all the consonant letters in your goal statement (all vowels are deleted), merged into one symbol. Then you put the sigil where you will see it each day.

Team Visioning

You can make the visioning process even more powerful by involving your team. Share with them your company vision, let them read the letter from your future self, show them your vision board. You could even put your vision board in a place where everyone on the team will see it every day.

Ask your team to do the exercise where they connect to their future self. For annual planning, that would be them+1 (them in one year's time). Have them each write out a letter from their future self saying who they are then, what they have achieved in the company and the exact steps they used to get there. As before, it is written in the past tense for a more certain energy. If they are visual people, then they can each create a vision board.

I have found staff to be energized by this exercise and effortlessly creating the results we want in the company during the year.

Magic Visions

Make your future letter or vision board even more powerful by adding intent to it. Get clear on what your intent for your vision is — for example, *"I create my goals this year with flow, ease, abundance and joy."* TLC yourself and TLC your future-self's letter or vision board. Then connect your heart to it and visualize your intent going into it.

You can also see your vision shining light into the world and easily creating itself during the year.

Adding magic and intent to your creations makes them appear in your business faster and with the energy that you add. Try it out on your next goals!

Short-Term Goals

You can use similar methods for 90-day plans, monthly goals and even weekly and daily goals.

I do TLC and visioning my day each morning after I have done yoga. Other people do it after running or swimming. The mind is quieter in the morning and it is easier to focus then.

You can also do a mini visioning session before a particular meeting or task, either using Meeting Magic (see chapter 5) or just asking "WWIT to easily and successfully complete this task?"

Creating Your Day

In your Office of the Mind (see Chapter 1), you can create the tasks you are going to do in your coming day. You can chose what kind of characteristics they will have — that you do them with ease, joy, success, profit, etc.

Visualize the tasks you are going to do and see them go by easily and effortlessly. Visualize each task written on a piece of paper on a table, and just see them just going by, as though the wind is blowing the pieces of paper off the table. When you do this, your days will be easy and productive. No stress. The right people will meet you at the right time. At the end of your day, you can feel grateful that "those tasks got completed easily."

You can also ask your intuition for inspirations on how to do tasks better. Ask "WWIT to have this task be successful, easy, and abundant for me?" Then listen for inspired ideas and actions that will achieve the task in these ways.

Not only does the WWIT clear the energy to make it happen easily, it also opens your mind to find solutions and ideas to help. For example, you could delegate this to someone else, or you could do it some other way, or whatever the inspiration is.

Affirmations

I recommend you write short affirmation essays instead of listing affirmations related to your mini-goals. When people think of affirmations, they usually write stuff like "I am a great marketer."

But research that has proven affirmations to be powerful asks participants to do something quite different. They write short essays (5 minutes is enough) explaining what's important to them, what their values are and why. So something more like "I am working on becoming a great marketer because I believe it allows me to reach people with an important message in a scalable way."

Doing this as part of your morning routine can help motivate you on your current mini-goals because it helps you remember why you are doing what you're doing.

If you feel the energy of plain affirmation compared to the energy of a short affirmation essay with your "whys" included, you will find that the second method has far more energy. It is more motivating for getting tasks done.

Notice that I write affirmations in the present rather than future tense. Example: "I will have a million-dollar business," versus "I have got a million-dollar business," has a real difference in energy. The second present tense version is more powerful because the thing in question is real when you say it in the present tense.

Remember your future self already has this result, so in a sense, it is true to say it.

Homeplay

- Visualize you+3 and write a letter from your future self.

- Name your future self (e.g., Super-Michael) and ask what your future self would do when you have challenges in your business.

- Make a vision board for your business goals with your team and keep it where all can see it.

Bonus Materials

The bonus materials from this chapter are at
www.intuitiveleadershipmastery.com/bonus/

- Create Your Year with Abundance with extra goal manifesting tools (video)

CHAPTER 9

Advanced Intuition Tools

"At times you have to leave the city of your comfort and go into the wilderness of your intuition. What you'll discover will be wonderful. What you'll discover is yourself." - *Alan Alda, actor, director, screenwriter, and author.*

Magic and Angels

I have used the phrase "business magic" in this book. We're obviously not talking about fairy tales here, so what does magic mean in this case? It means that you manipulate what is happening in your business by changing the energy of a situation.

How do you do that?

You TLC (To the Light, Connect). You throw light into the pattern, you clear stuff from the youngest age you recall this situation arising, you use WWIT (What Would It Take). Those are all ways to use magic.

Now, you already use magic in your business — you just don't call it magic. You use it when you create a vision for your business, when you leverage branding to turn prospects into customers, or when you motivate staff to give their best. It's any time you shift the energy of a situation to get what you want.

You set a clear intention and use some spiritual tool to help manifest what you want. You might do a visualization, a WWIT, some kind of clearing, or asking angels to help.

Yes, I said you can ask angels to help you with business problems. Angels are waiting to help you as soon as you ask, but if you don't ask them for anything, they won't help. One of their primary rules is not to assist unless explicitly requested. They don't want to interfere in your life if it's unwelcome, so in the following exercise, we are going to look at how to ask for an angel gift for your business.

Angel Gift Exercise:

- Say: *"I want an angel to come in front of me that's going to help me with this (sale/hire/business issue)."*

- Put your hand out, palm facing up, and ask for a gift from them.

- After a few seconds, you may feel some energy shift in your hand.

   - It might get hot or cold, tingly, or some other sensation.

- Then ask what you got in your hand. Describe it if you can.

   - You may get information about what the gift it is. You might get, *"This is a golden box that contains extra courage to help you sell better"* or a knife to cut through a difficult problem, or something else.

   - How might that help you in your situation?

- ○ In some situations, you may not get intuitive information, but you still feel something there. It is unknown to you in the present moment.

- Then see where you are drawn to put the gift in your body.

- ○ Heart? Head? Stomach? Somewhere else? Put it wherever your intuition leads you to put it. If you don't hear your intuition this time then just put the gift in your heart.

- Notice how you feel.

This is what CEO Willo O'Brien said on receiving an angel gift in one of my intuition workshops about helping a client of hers who was in great pain:

"What I really see and sense is I can go so directly to her pain and her struggle that I instantly, as soon as you even asked this angel to come, it was (that) I want to surround her with this light and these angels, and support her through seeing this choice, this step, this opportunity."

Another way you can ask your angels to help is to ask them for specific guidance on a question you have. For example, if you're hiring — "Hey, Angels, can you tell me which of these candidates I should hire that would really help my business in this particular way?" or "Angel, which candidate would be ideal?"

If you are not already working with your angels and guides, that does not mean you don't have any. It is either that you are not asking for help from them or you are not listening to the messages they are giving you. In the latter case, if you want to change and hear those messages, you could ask:

- WWIT (What Would It Take) to connect with my angels and guides?

- WWIT (What Would It Take) to be cool with talking with angels?

Spiritual Advisory Board

Why not add some of your angels to your Spiritual Advisory Board? (See the chapter on the Intuition Toolkit for details of your Spiritual Advisory Board. It is a group of spiritual beings in your Office of the Mind that you can ask advice and help from.)

Tip: You don't have to stay with the guides you already have.

You can update your Board with new members anytime you want. You're not stuck with the angels and guides you had several years ago. Some people think, "Oh, angels are wonderful. If I invite them into my life, then I have to obey them all the time." That's not the case. They're here to benefit us. While angels have their own purposes, if they are going to be part of your life, then they need to be beneficial to you.

You can ask your intuition:

- Are all my guides of a high vibration (love or higher on the Hawkins scale)?

- How many are of a lower vibration?

- How many are not beneficial for me personally?

Any that are not high vibration or beneficial to you are potentially off the Board. You can either command them to leave, or you can TLC (To the Light, Connect) them and use WWIT to see if you can upgrade them.

In the case of guides that are of dead people, you can command them to go to The Light. (Often they are afraid of going to The Light but are attached to your light, particularly as you TLC more.

You can help them overcome their fear of going to the light and help them upgrade their vibration.) Once they have gone to the light, they can come back with a higher vibration and may be a better fit for your new Spiritual Advisory Board.

You may have other low vibration entities of dead people hanging around you, draining your energy and feeding off your addictions and business drama. These I recommend sending to the light the same way. Removing entities from you, your business and your staff can totally change the vibration, joy and results in a business.

Intuition Gym

Intuition is just like a muscle. The more we use it and work it, the more we exercise it, the stronger it's going to be.

You need a "'gym" for your intuition. Do a daily intuition workout.

There are many different ways to use your intuition each day. I like the Office of the Mind visualization or using any intuitive tools daily such as TLC or WWIT can also be useful.

- WWIT to work out your intuition every day?
- WWIT to use your intuition 10 times every day?

What If You're Blocked on Visualizing?

Some people are blocked on visualizing. They just have difficulty with that, but they hear intuition or they feel the messages instead. People frequently ask whether you have to actually be able to *see* the Office of the Mind, or if they might just hear their guides or get a "'felt sense" in the body of what they're saying.

Intuition comes in a multitude of ways. If you're a visual learner or thinker, then you're more likely to see imagery in your mind. If you're auditory, you're likely to hear it, and you'll probably feel your intuition physically if you're kinesthetic.

Turning Up Your Intuition Volume

How can you turn up the volume on your intuition, so you can receive it better?

- Meditation, because you're quieting your mind.

- Prayer, because you are asking for help.

- Living a balanced life. That means not working sixteen hours a day, seven days a week and destroying other parts of your life such as your relationships or health.

All these things give you more space and time to hear your intuition.

When you are so "'in your mind" all the time, focusing on just work or some other addiction, you cannot hear your intuition easily. There's just too much external information crammed into your head and body for intuitive messages to make it to the surface where you can find them.

To check your life balance, I recommend an evaluation called the Wheel of Life, and a similar tool called the Wheel of Business for your work. You can download spreadsheets and graphs for these from the book bonus website www.intuitiveleadershipmastery.com/bonus/.

When your Wheel of Life is not balanced, you tend to have a bumpy ride — rather like riding on a bicycle when one of the wheels is bent out of shape.

The more content and balanced you are in life, the more space you tend to have to hear your intuition. You have a time to work, a time to be with friends or family, a time to be social, a time to exercise your body or eat well, and you have the time to connect with the spiritual side of yourself.

Prayers and Goals

Prayers can be requests to a god, your angels or intuition. Or they can be saying gratitudes that you have for them for the ways that they will help you or have already helped you.

There are many forms for praying. This is how CEO Chris Reynolds told me that he prays:

> *"In the evenings, what I do is I'll get down, and actually I guess it's a Christian form of prayer, but I'll get down on the side of my bed and bow on my knees and just put my arms on the bed. I just say what I'm grateful for for the day and in my life. Then I'll send some prayers out to people that need a good prayer or a good thought. I pray for my business, the people that are affected by my business. I pray for the DC, the people that are at the events in the DC, the people that I'm surrounding myself with at the time, family members that are sick or passing or just need some good thoughts.*
>
> *Then I talk to God quite a bit and I consider God more like a brother or a best friend as opposed to a father-figure. For me, God's like a partner in my creation for what I want to create*

in this world. That's part of the intuitive communication because sometimes I'm like... I call God dude sometimes, or buddy or whatever. I'm like, "Hey, dude, what should we do right now?" I just think in my mind what would feel right to do.

I see God as an actual physical brother or best friend to where we can just banter back and forth about shit. Sometimes I get pissed off at him and cuss him, and sometimes he just laughs and whatever. He sweats it off like it's nothing."

(The DC is an abbreviation for Dynamite Circle, a group of abundance focused, location independent entrepreneurs.)

What Would God Do? You can ask yourself this anytime you have a business problem. Or invite God into your Spiritual Advisory Board.

Really God — however you think of God — is everything. You. Me. All the billions of humans. Animals. Plants. Rocks. Planets. Stars. Space. Your business.

All of our reality.

And at the same time, God has split up all these pieces of our reality so we have a myriad of different experiences, from every point of view. It is like a hologram — if you break a hologram into pieces, each piece has all the information of the whole but with lower resolution.

Traditionally, many people see God as some guy up in heaven playing chess with our lives. Like the Greek god Zeus saying *"I'm going to move you this way and I'm going to tease you a little bit and give you a bad business situation and laugh at you when you don't do what I think is right."*

But my view is that God is not separate from us. You are God. And the whole of God is here as a co-creator or partner in our life and business. It can guide us if we listen.

God Experiencing Everything

Let's take that a step further. God is in everything, including each of us. Each of us is God with a body on this planet in this time-slice that we're in.

So when we experience something in our life, God is experiencing that, and that's part of the point. Before the universe was created, it was just spiritual energy and it wasn't divided up into different pieces and types. It was a different kind of experience. God could experience what it's like to be in a body on a planet. That's how come we're incarnated here, so we are different little holographic pieces of the God-force, and we're having all our experiences so that we can experience the stuff that you can't experience in a spiritual realm.

Undoing Victimhood: *The Little Soul In The Sun*

Many entrepreneurs go into the victim state a lot of times and they'll say, "Why me?" They start blaming others or God for things that are going wrong in their lives and businesses. This blocks your intuition and limits your ability to see your way forward.

What if, instead of searching for someone to blame, you realized that you had chosen your problems before you incarnated so that you could have certain experiences and growth? What if you chose these problems and now you're getting the exact lessons you need to progress to what you really want in life?

This is a theme explored in the short book *"The Little Soul in the Sun"* by famous spiritual teacher Neale Donald Walsch (author of *"Conversations with God"*). *The Little Soul* is written as a children's book, but it's really good for adults.

The Little Soul is in Heaven with other souls (spirits), deciding on his next incarnation, and he says, "This time around I really want to experience something a bit more meaty in my incarnation. I'd like to experience deep betrayal."

"But I can't do it on my own. And I can't do it with my usual high vibration. Is there anyone else up here in Heaven that will incarnate down with me and really screw me over?" Someone else says, "I love you so much, Little Soul. I will lower my vibration so that I will be able to do that for you. But I'm a little concerned that I might forget that I'm a spiritual being when I'm incarnated down on Earth. Will anyone else come down with us to remind both of us that we're both spiritual beings having a human experience, not humans having a spiritual experience?"

All three of them incarnate down onto Earth. They have the betrayal, the Little Soul gets to experience this emotion, an experience they've never had before, and they're all happy spirits in the end.

I love this story because it gives such perspective to the situations we create in our lives.

There's no need to create victimhood or suffering in our life or business. That's a meaning we put on those experiences, not the experience itself. Changing your perspective like this when things get hard can turn your troubles into freedom and momentum in an instant.

What is Struggle?

There is a lot of narrative in our culture about struggle, that life is ultimately suffering. But when you struggle in your work, it's not that the work itself is too hard or too heavy — it's that humans are wired to layer story, emotion and meaning on top of our tasks.

Struggle is a choice. If you struggle in your business, you probably have a belief that work is supposed to be hard, that other people are against you, and that only by hard work and suffering can you succeed. Maybe you heard over and over that money doesn't grow on trees, that life's a bitch and then you die, or that the only way to get out of the gutter is to work your way up by any means possible.

You might have been taught that money is the root of all evil (when, in fact, that quote from the Bible is that the *love of money* — craving it, being unable to separate your own personal worth from your dollar value — is the root of all evil). Maybe you believe that business is not spiritual, or that it is cheating to use spiritual tools to make work easier.

If any of these beliefs resonate with you, then I recommend making a list of beliefs you want to clear and using some of the tools from this book to help. Look at the The Work of Byron Katie tool (Chapter 2) or the Youngest Age Pattern Recycling tool (also Chapter 2).

Consciously Creating Your Day

If you use the tools in this book to create your day, then you can avoid victimhood and struggle in your business. Consciously creating your day means that you set an intention for your day and use spiritual tools to create it the way you want it to be. It can be really joyful and smooth and abundant. Your work can be effortless, your team can be effective and cohesive, and you can find balance in your life.

Three tools that are particularly useful in creating your day are:

- TLC (To the Light, Connect)
- WWIT (What Would It Take)
- Office of the Mind

You can use them separately or together.

Here's what it looks like separately:

TLC: You TLC yourself and then say your tasks for the day. Preferably in the past tense (see Chapter 8 (Visioning) for why).

WWIT: For each task ask, "WWIT to complete this task successfully with ease and joy?" (I add the WWIT modifiers of ease and joy because that will give you inspired actions. This means that not only will you get the task done, but it will be easy and fun for you. That avoids creating struggle in your tasks.)

Office of the Mind: You can discuss your tasks for the day with your Spiritual Advisory Board to get ideas for doing them easily. You can also do a visualization there called Task Running. Visualize each task on a piece of paper in a stack and have your fingers run over the papers like they're little horses or mice that are running down a track, pushing all the papers quickly behind them, getting them done easily and effortlessly.

Using the tools together looks like this:

First TLC. Then go to your Office of the Mind and ask your Spiritual Advisory Board for each task: WWIT to complete this task successfully with ease and joy? Note any inspired actions you get. You can also do the Task Running visualization on your task list.

Another tool you can use is to feel down your to-do list for any items that contain struggle or pain. Either feel down the list until your fingers feel a sticky item, or look at where your eyes are attracted to. When you first experiment with this method, you might turn your to-do list upside down so you cannot unconsciously read the items. You can either work with a handwritten list, a printout or on your computer screen.

When you find a sticky item, use the tools to clear the struggle pattern from the task. You could TLC, then see light coming from above and below into the task. Or notice how you feel thinking about doing the task and clear the emotions and body responses that come up with the Pattern Recycling tool. Or ask WWIT to do this task with ease and joy? Just asking this WWIT starts clearing a struggle pattern in the task.

Note that you can use all the same methods for creating your week, quarter, year, decade, or lifetime.

Animal Symbols

Intuitive messages may come to you via animal symbols. If you notice an animal in an unusual place or time or having weird behavior, then it may be a message from your intuition. By animal I am including mammals, reptiles, birds or insects here — any living creature.

Note down what animal you saw, how many you saw, what they were doing, which direction they were traveling and any intuitive impressions you got from the experience. You can Google the animal's name and totem to see common messages from that animal (e.g., Google "snake totem" and see what comes up).

For example, one year I was on a yoga retreat in the mountains of New Mexico and I saw a 3-foot-long snake in the path I was walking along. She was totally relaxed, sunning herself on the ground. This was unusual as I had been there many times and had never seen a snake — they usually stay away from humans. One of the meanings of snakes is transformation, because they shed their skin as they grow. At the time I was doing a lot of personal growth and had a cold. Seeing the snake reminded me that I was going through a transformation and that everything was okay, even if it didn't feel like it at the time.

If you want to read more details on the meanings of animal signs, the book "Animals Speak" by Ted Andrews is very good. It includes common animal signs, as well as the meanings of the number of animals and directions in which they are moving.

Intuitively Picking Successful Company and Product Names

If you are picking a product or a company name, then look at the energy that it has in it.

You can use the Two Chairs Method (see Chapter 5) to read the energy of a name that you are considering. Imagine that the name is another spiritual being with a body. You are an observer and your ideal client is in one chair facing the product name you are reading in the second chair.

Notice how both your ideal client and the product name look. What size are their heads, bodies, legs? Do each of them have feet? Where are they looking? What color(s) are they? With the intuitive information that you receive, you can use your intuition to interpret what it means about this product name and your ideal client.

You can use Joy and Profit Graphs (see Chapter 5) to predict how much joy and profit a particular name will have over time. Perhaps the Profit Graph starts off negative, then spikes up. That might indicate that you have to invest in marketing the name until sales take off. Or perhaps the graph ends after two years — that might indicate that the product dies after that amount of time.

You can also use the numerology of the name to see what energy it contains. Refer to a book on numerology on how to do this, or you can have the professional astrology of a product or company done for you by an astrologer. They will want to know the exact location that you are creating the product or company at (the place of "birth") and the exact date/time you will create it (the time of "birth"). Obviously the place and time are under your control, so you can discuss with your astrologer where and when are best for creating this new name.

The date of a company is usually taken to be its incorporation date/time. And the date of a product might be the date/time of your first sale. If you need a particular date/time, then a friend can make the purchase to help you get started.

In many countries such as China, business people commonly, deliberately form a company on a certain date and time and place for this very reason, and use or avoid certain numbers for greater fortune and luck in business.

Alternatively, if you already have a particular product name or business name in use, you can use your intent to create the energy you desire for it, thereby overcoming the numerology or astrology that are inherent in it. Remember we are all God with a body, so anything is possible.

I think of astrology as being similar to the weather forecast. If rain is forecast when I want to walk, I can choose to bring an umbrella with me to stay dry, although this is harder than just saving the walk for a sunny day. So I recommend you go with the good astrological days when you are creating something in your business when you can. That way, you can use your energy for other tasks. However, if that is not convenient, you can add your intent to the name.

To do this, TLC (To the Light, Connect), then use WWIT or Meeting Magic (Chapter 1) to set your intent for the name. For example, if your product is called Alpha and you want it to attract ideal clients and to be perceived as fun and useful for them, then ask:

- WWIT for Alpha to attract ideal clients and be seen as fun and useful by them?

Similarly with Meeting Magic, put Alpha in the room and throw the words "attract ideal clients and be seen as fun and useful" into it when you do the visualization.

Case Study: Clearing Lack of Focus in Business

I worked with CEO Louise Cottrell during a workshop. She just started a new business and was feeling overwhelmed with different tasks she thought that she should be doing. She lacked clarity and focus and so was not making headway on any tasks. In this case study, we use the following two tools:

- Youngest Age Pattern Recycling tool from Chapter 6
- Spread out the cards reduce overwhelm tool (introduced below)

You can find the video of this case study in the book bonus resources at www.intuitiveleadershipmastery.com/bonus/

Michael: Louise, what's the issue you have in your business you want to work on?

Louise: I don't know where to focus. My business is relatively new. There are too many things. I only have so much energy. I have a list of a hundred things I can do, and I don't know which would be the most beneficial.

Michael: You don't know where to focus. What do you feel in your body when you think about this?

Louise: Hesitance. Hesitation and overwhelmed.

Michael: Confused, overwhelmed.

Louise: Confusion, cloudy ... cloudy brain.

Michael: What do you physically notice in your body? Any bits tense, fuzzy, hot, cold? Any other sensations?

Louise: The pit of my stomach is heavy.

(Note: We are going to use the Youngest Age Pattern Recycling tool from Chapter 6 here)

Michael: The pit of your stomach is heavy. Let's TLC - connect to the light. Let's go up, go down. Expand your heart out. Let's send light to your stomach. What's the youngest age you felt the same way, where you were confused, overwhelmed, the pit of your stomach was heavy?

Louise: Two.

Michael: Who was that with?

Louise: Mother.

Michael: Do you consciously remember what happened?

Note: It doesn't matter if you do or not — just go with the first age and person that you get from your intuition.

Louise: No.

Michael: Let's send light to your two-year-old self with her mother where she (your two-year-old self) had a tummy that was tight. She was confused, overwhelmed. Let's send love and light to every other age where you recreated this pattern.

When you have something in your childhood and you create a pattern from them like Louise has, you tend to recreate it in your life until you heal it. For example, with relationships — you have some screw-up in your life so you attract a boyfriend or girlfriend who really hurts you. Either you heal it then, or you date someone else who's the same way.

You keep repeating that until you heal it. Same thing in business. You either keep repeating the pattern in your business where you're confused and overwhelmed and have a heavy tummy, or you heal it and you're done and never have to repeat it again.

How are you doing now, Louise? How do you feel now? Can you think about the issue you told us, about what you're going to do in your business?

Louise: Yeah.

Michael: What do you notice now?

Louise: Speaking.

Michael: What does speaking mean?

Louise: I feel called to speak.

Louise: You feel called to speak. How's your tummy?

Louise: Good.

Michael: How's the clarity of your head?

Louise: Good. I feel a concern about having to hack away at stuff, but I know that's the easy part.

Michael: It's too many things to do or something?

Louise: It's too many ideas. Too many potentials.

Michael: Let's imagine all the potentials in front of you, like cards on a table. They're a little clustered together, and let's spread them out a bit. Let's have the three ideas that are the top ones to do right now. Let's have them shine out to you so they light up. Now how do you feel about speaking and doing this? All right. Good. Let's share in the Facebook group how this works out for you.

Louise: Okay.

Michael: I think you're still unfolding this, and I think most of it's fixed. That's what I get. How do you feel?

Louise: Like I have a direction I can go in.

Michael: Okay. It sounds like you'd like to say that with certainty.

Louise: Yes!

Check in two weeks later:
Michael: How are you doing on the issue we worked on?

Louise: Where to focus keeps changing, but the drain on my energy is no longer an issue! I'm working with a business coach now on an entirely different way to structure my business which is more focused and will take less work.

What I realized is that it didn't even matter what the "answer" is, just that the energy is cleared.

Case Study: Working with Your Angels

I interviewed Brazilian CEO Nicole Seelinger about how she works with her angels.

How do you connect with your angels?

> "When I'm in a highly stressful situation and my brain is working too much sometimes I have difficulty meditating. In moments that I feel like I'm not able to connect with myself and get the answers from my inner wisdom, then I'll ask for help. I really like looking at the skies and stars, and just talk with the sky sometimes or talk with the angels saying, "Where should I go? I don't know anymore how to solve this. What is the path that I should take right now because it's really blurry. I don't know what is the best way to move on.""

Do you say this out loud or in your head or do you write it down?

> "I think people have different ways of doing it. Writing is a very powerful way to set our goals out and to say what we want. That's a way to start materializing, but in my case, I just say it out loud, or if I'm talking with the universe, if

there is no one around me, I'll say it out loud. If there are people around me, I'll just say it in my head."

Do you hear answers immediately, or in the next day? How long does it take?

"Not immediately. Sometimes I feel I can already start feeling a bit of peace and calm. That comes immediately, that whatever it is is going to work out. The answers tend to come really quick later on the same day or even the next day. Sometimes everything changes completely, in a way that is surprising. All the pieces of a puzzle come together and it can be very impressive."

Sounds like a powerful thing to have in your business. You mentioned a story where your guides and angels helped you out getting a visa. Can you share that with us?

"I had many opportunities. I had an invitation to go to a 'workation' in Romania, and friends were getting married in Romania as well, but I just couldn't say yes. I had to wait for the appointment for the visa that would be somewhere around Europe.

I also had at the same time to get my passport renewed and that would have to be in the Brazilian embassy. I had to wait for answers from 2 different embassies from 2 different countries that probably would be based in 2 different countries. I had to somehow make it happen together.

The embassy, for example, for renewing the visa, some needed appointment and they would take me in about 1 month. Some I could just show up, but it would take me 60 days to have it back. Some they would just cut my passport and I wouldn't be able to even travel. I was emailing and calling more than 10 embassies around Europe to try to find out how I would do this.

There was a point that I was just really exhausted with it all. My friend wanted to know if I would come to her wedding. The girl from the workation, who invited me to go to the mountains in Romania, she wanted, of course, to know if she could count on me. I was just feeling so frustrated and so exhausted and completely out of control of my life.

I remember this day that I was really exhausted and I was just like, "Come on, please. I know everything is going to be fine, but can you please hurry up in getting me the answer because I cannot take it. I'm tired of not knowing what's going on, where should I go, how I should arrange this. I need to get out of the Schengen zone, I need to work, and make this visa thing happen. I need to renew my passport. There are too many variables that are right now pieces of a puzzle and I don't know how to connect them. Where should I go?"

Just to be clear to the readers, you were talking to your angels and guides at that point?

"I was talking to the universe. I also asked my angels, "Please show me ... Can you just guide me because right now I'm

tired." I was trying to keep looking for flights, and I just couldn't even book anything. I'm very flexible, but sometimes I go to an extreme so that I just have no clue of what I'm doing next, no clue at all of what I'm going to be even in the next 2 days or something.

In that moment I was just having a break down. I was like, "Can you just please, please ... I'm really tired ... I closed the computer. I was like, "I'm not going to think about this any more ... Just show me what to do, where to go, how does that all comes together.

The next day, I had a confirmation of an appointment on the Czech Republic embassy in Vienna right before the workation in Romania. I had as well finally the reply from the embassy in Bucharest, which was pretty much the best and easiest way to get a new passport for me. It was perfect because I could just go on the way, go to Vienna and then from Vienna go to the workation.

Everything would work out because I would be outside Schengen. I could go to the wedding. I could go visit a friend as well in Bulgaria. It was awesome. On the workation as well, I connected with many people, many friends from before, made connections for the future as well. Everything got together in a way that I would never be able to put it together like that."

That's a powerful method if you're feeling overwhelmed with too much information, too many options, to just ask

the universe or ask your angels and guides to help you to take it easy.

> "I think so. It's not about just asking and not doing anything. Let's just remember that I was going crazy. I had already emailed about 13 embassies or something like that. I had called a few of them. I was really doing my homework.
>
> I was really doing everything already. I think it's about the acknowledgement that sometimes there are plans like that. We don't really know what's best for us and maybe something that we are not predicting can just be arranged. I think it's about trusting."

Clearing Limiting Beliefs

Our limiting beliefs affect how well our business will do because we have things that we want to do in our business, but we hold ourselves back. We have resistance.

Where does this resistance come from? We grow up having a lot of input from society, especially from our parents and from our closest friends. We pick up their beliefs and make them our own. Then we have these beliefs in our core. Beliefs such as "Money is evil," or, "I cannot show up too much. I need to be humble."

The case of CEO Nicole Seelinger, from the story above, is typical. She told me that:

> "This was mainly the energy of my mom getting into my head. Because of that, even though I was doing a lot of things in my business, I always avoided speaking in public. I would

just shake if I would talk in public. If I was in front of a camera, even worse. I would not be able to do an interview for my business.

About 2 years ago, I realized that this was why my business was not working. Because I was afraid of speaking, of putting myself out there, of even blogging about it. I was like, 'No, I cannot do this. I cannot speak in front of people. I just shake.'"

We have an invisible world of beliefs behind the reality of our business. All the things that we believe there manifest in our visible world because we make decisions based on our beliefs. Our actions are based on our beliefs.

To find out what limiting beliefs you have, think about a goal that you are resisting working on or completing. Then think about what beliefs would support that resistance. Then think about your parents when you were a child. How did they act towards that topic?

For example, how did your parents act around money? Did they spend a lot of money in a careless way and now you are afraid of spending and save so much that you lose out on opportunities? Or were they very religious and thought that money is evil and said things like, "People that have too much money are selfish or evil"? And because of this you think, "I don't want money." I've heard so many entrepreneurs say things such as "I don't want to grow my business too much. I don't need money. I don't want the money."

One way to release these limiting beliefs is to create three beliefs for each one of the limiting beliefs that you have, as an antidote for the negative beliefs.

For example, if you believe, "I don't need money because money is evil," you could create these three antidote beliefs:

- "Money is good."

- "Money is neutral."

- "I need money and with it, I can do good things for me and others."

Change your perception of money. Money is just a tool. It is a tool for materializing things on Earth. However you use it is just an expression of yourself in that moment. If you use it for good, you might think of it as good. If you use it for bad, you might think of it as bad. Money is neutral.

Money is not evil. It takes on the meaning you ascribe to it.

The other tools mentioned earlier in this chapter help in clearing limiting beliefs, too.

This is powerful because so many business people have limiting beliefs. Whether you call them negative patterns, blind spots, destructive tendencies, we all have them. Some of us just put in the work to unravel them and let our intuition shine through in their place.

Why do we have so many programs that make us feel weak? Because we are most scared about how powerful we really are underneath. Afraid that others might not love us if we show how powerful we really are.

"Our deepest fear is that we are powerful beyond measure. It is our light, not our darkness that most frightens us. Your playing small does not serve the world. There is nothing

enlightened about shrinking so that other people won't feel insecure around you." - Marianne Williamson, author and speaker

Anywhere in your business that isn't working well, or that has plateaued, is usually where you will find your limiting beliefs.

Plateaus are a particularly common problem in business. Everything starts out well, you grow the business to a certain level, and then things flatten off. If you check with the founder, they often have beliefs such as: "I can only grow up to this point. I just need this amount of revenue a month," or, "I cannot handle too many people, to have a big team."

No business will ever outgrow their founder. Either the founder will have to step aside so a new CEO can take charge so the business can grow, or the founder needs to speed up their personal growth. Otherwise, the business will stop at some point and reach a plateau. Or worse, it will collapse.

That is why this inner work is so important.

Clearing Depression and Entities.

Feeling depressed is common in entrepreneurs. But have you asked if this energy is yours or someone else's? Often emotions are not even ours! This is especially true for people sensitive to energy, as many business leaders naturally are.

If you get a "no" from your intuition when you ask if it is your energy, then you can tell it to leave you. TLC, then command it. "What is mine is mine and what is yours is yours. Leave now!"

You don't have to know what particular person it is from. Sometime I feel sadness from the whole town I am in... But when I become conscious that it is not my emotion and ask it to leave, then I feel better.

Also, I recommend removing all entities you have around you. Be sure to check under your feet, over your head, behind you and inside your body in addition to the usual places outside your body. Then TLC and command them to leave, sending them to the light.

You can ask your intuition: "How many entities are around me now?" before and after sending the ones you find to the light. Be sure to heal the parts of your body where they were sucking your energy. These are the places that hold that pattern that allowed them to stay without you noticing them before. That way, new ones can't come back.

Also clear all entities in your house, car and office. You send entities to the light by commanding them to "Go to the light."

Chakra Cleaning

Chakras are energy centers in the body. After years without any cleaning, they are often blocked and can reduce the amount of energy you have for your work. Regular cleaning both gives you more energy and makes you more vibrant to your clients and staff.

There are 7 chakras in the body. They are:

- The Root chakra, at the base of the spine, responsible for a sense of being grounded
- The Sacral chakra, in the lower abdomen, responsible for our ability to connect with others and new experiences

- The Solar Plexus chakra, in the stomach area, responsible for a sense of confidence and control

- The Heart chakra, in the heart area, responsible for our ability to love and be loved

- The Throat chakra, in the throat area, responsible for our ability to clearly communicate

- The Third Eye chakra, in the forehead area between the eyes, responsible for focus and perception

- The Crown chakra, on the top of the head, responsible for our spiritual growth and capacity for bliss.

To clean your chakras:

- Connect to the light above and below and expand your heart energy.

- Focus on each chakra in turn and intuit what condition it is in: color, size, mess? What shape and color does it want to be for you to be happy and healthy (or whatever energy state you want to be in)? WWIT for it to be in that shape and color?

- Are there any old emotions stuck in it? Delete them.

- Are there any cords or other psychic objects or entities in it? Cut them and send to the light.

- Be sure to check both the front and back of chakra.

- Repeat for all chakras. You can do the 7 ones in the body (root, sacral, solar, heart, throat, third eye, crown) plus the earth star and soul star.

- If you feel drawn to clear other minor chakras such as hands, feet, ankles, knees, etc., clean them, too.

I either do this myself in a meditative space, or lying in bed after waking or before sleep for 10-45 minutes. Or I listen to a guided meditation that clears chakras for 45 minutes.

Homeplay

- Experiment with asking for and receiving Angel Gifts.
- Invite one of your Angels on to your Spiritual Advisory Board for a week, as an experiment. Notice the quality of the business advice that you get.
- Take 5 minutes of quiet time for yourself today. Notice how your day goes afterwards.
- Experiment with having a struggle-free day at work today. WWIT?
- Consciously Creating your day each day for a week as an experiment. Notice how your days go.
- Play with adding your intent to your company name. Notice how you feel and how your reality shifts.

Bonus Materials

The bonus materials from this chapter are at www.intuitiveleadershipmastery.com/bonus/

- Clearing lack of focus in business (audio)
- Wheel of Life and Wheel of Business (spreadsheets)

CHAPTER 10

Summary

M any business leaders use their intuition to make more profits and reduce stress. But they keep this method to themselves, often unintentionally, and don't know how to expand their intuition skills. With the tools in this book you have learned how to increase your business intuition and with it, your profits and joy.

This is is critical given the exponential increasing pace of change in the modern world. Rational decision-making methods are no longer enough, and it's more important than ever to see clearly what's in front of you.

TLC and WWIT are the foundational tools for developing your intuition. If you only use these two tools everyday in your business you will get amazing results:

- TLC (To the Light, Connect) visualisation exercise. Open the mind and heart to intuitive inspiration. Being in a positive, open, solution-oriented emotional space is crucial to accessing your inner genius.

- Asking WWIT (What Would It Take) to achieve X (and being open to the answers). I love this question. It can help you set more exciting goals and focus on creating big wins in your business.

Other important intuition tools are:

- Intuition Journal. Keep a journal of intuitive decisions that can be reviewed periodically to track the effectiveness of intuitive decision making vs rational methods.

- Future self. Visualizing yourself in the future, and asking your future self how they got where they are.

- Spiritual Advisory Board. A board of advisors in your Office of the Mind who you can ask for business advice. Can include living, dead, future or imaginary people; angels or guides.

- Joy and Profit graphs. Imagine what these graphs look like in the future for hires, clients and teams.

- Two chairs method. Imagine yourself in one chair and the person or thing you want to get intuitive info in the other chair.

- Youngest Age Pattern Recycling. Used to clear self-sabotaging patterns from you in your business.

These tools are applicable to all areas of your business: hiring, sales, marketing, visioning, teams, IT, accounting, legal and more.

They become even more powerful when you share these tools with your staff, clients and vendors, empowering them to use their intuition to help build your business, and to help them grow more themselves.

Only by this shift to the open use of intuition and magic in business can we navigate the increasing chaos and opportunity in the world.

Let's make the world a much better place for everyone to live in. WWIT?

- Michael Light, January 2017.

Bonus Materials

You can take your business intuition skills to the next level with the book bonus materials at
www.intuitiveleadershipmastery.com/bonus/

- WWIT cheat sheet (doc)

CHAPTER 11

Resources

Books

- "Beyond Human" by Jaden Rose Phoenix

- "What Do You Mean the Third Dimension is Going Away?" by Jim Self

- "Animal Speak: The Spiritual & Magical Powers of Creatures Great and Small" by Ted Andrews

- "Busting Loose From the Money Game: Mind-Blowing Strategies for Changing the Rules of a Game You Can't Win" by Robert Scheinfeld

- "Matrix Energetics: The Science and Art of Transformation" by Richard Bartlett

- "Practical Intuition" by Laura Day

- "Blink" by Malcolm Gladwell

- "Creating Money: Attracting Abundance" by Duane Packer and Sanaya Roman

- "Maverick: The success story behind the world's most unusual workplace" by Ricardo Semler

- "The Inevitable: Understanding the 12 Technological Forces That Will Shape Our Future" by Kevin Kelly

- "The End of Jobs: Money, Meaning and Freedom Without the 9-to-5" by Taylor Pearson

- "The Little Soul in the Sun" by Neale Donald Walsch

Healers, Coaches and Teachers

- Brad Blanton, Radical Honesty http://radicalhonesty.com/

- Christie Marie Sheldon, Love or Above, Unlimited Abundance, Intuitive Life Coach Training http://christiesheldon.com/

- Cindy Sheldon Brown, Intuitive Life Coach http://www.cindyabrown.com/

- DeAnn Scheppele, Inspirational Coach http://deannscheppele.com/

- Guru Dev Singh, Sat Nam Rasayan http://www.gurudevsnr.com/

- Jacki Beem, Energy healer http://hiwattliving.com/

- Jaden Phoenix, Holographic Healing http://www.alchemywisdom.com/

- Joan Newcomb, Mystic Mentorship http://www.joannewcomb.com/

- John Armitage, Multi Dimensional Transformation http://www.new-paradigm-mdt.org/

- Justice Bartlett Conscious Trance-Form Play http://www.playfullyconscious.com/

- Kam Yuen, Yuen Method http://yuenmethod.com/

- Kasha-Shana Turner, Intuitive Coach & Consciousness Facilitator http://kasha-shana.com/

- Lisa C. Anderson, Intuitive Energy Coach, http://www.The-Healers-Healer.com/

- Mark Dunn, Conscious Systems http://www.conscioussystems.net/

- Raven Dana, Graphologist, Stress Wizard www.stresswizardcoaching.com

- Richard Bartlett, Matrix Energetics https://www.matrixenergetics.com/

- Robin Wolfson, Consciousness Coaching http://www.newrealitiesgroup.com/

- Susan Campbell, Getting Real, Communication Coach http://www.susancampbell.com/

- Terry Brussell-Gibbons, Hypnotherapist http://www.acesuccess.com/

- Yogi Bhajan https://www.3ho.org/

Bonus Materials

The bonus spreadsheets, video and audio for the book are at www.intuitiveleadershipmastery.com/bonus/

Gratitudes

I am grateful to the following people who helped in creating this book.

- Book details
  - Inspiration and WWIT answers: My intuition
  - Structural Editor and Book Coach: Laura Hanly http://laurahanly.com/
  - Copy Editor: Lisa C. Anderson
  - Marketing: Judy Schramm and Paul Zivotic
  - Executive Assistant: El Princess Eclar
  - Photographer: Lauren Schneider
  - Cover design: Milica Zivotic
  - Sound Engineer: Christopher Lang
  - Website: Douglas Yuen https://efficientwp.com/
- Coaches, Teachers and Healers I have worked with over many years:
  - Brad Blanton, Christie Marie Sheldon, Cindy Sheldon Brown, Darshan Kaur, DeAnn Scheppele, Glory Lane, Guru Dev Singh, Jacki Beem, Jaden Phoenix, Joan Newcomb, John Armitage, Justice Bartlett, Kam Yuen, Kasha-Shana Turner, Lisa C. Anderson, Mark Dunn, Millie Knox, Raven Dana, Richard Bartlett, Robin Wolfson, Stefanie Müller, Susan Campbell, Terry Brussell-Gibbons, Yogi Bhajan.
- The Dynamite Circle, which has provided an abundant group of location independent entrepreneurs to share these tools with over the past few years and get feedback.

- <u>Entrepreneur House</u> Barcelona, where I set the goals for this book.

- All the beta readers in the Conscious CEO Growth group, especially top commenters:

  - Mandi Ellefson, Barbara Fernandez, Viktor Ilijev, Eli David, Judy Schramm, Gabby Wallace, Kundan Chhabra, Mariza Leal, Willo O'Brien, Yamile Yemoonyah, Elies Hadi, Judy Schramm, Gabby Wallace, Cody McKibben, Vivien Chen, Dustin Overbeck, Bee Kal and Christopher Sutton

- Everyone who has attended my workshops and webinars over the years.

- All the interviewees for the <u>Intuitive Leadership Mastery podcast:</u>

  - Amanda Cook, Anita Strittmatter, Chris Reynolds, Dan Norris, David Schneider, Elaine Nieberding, Euvie Ivanova, Gabrielle Wallace, John Wingate, Karsten Aichholz, Kristen Yates, Kundan Chhabra, Louise C, Mads Singers, Mandi Ellefson, Michael Gurevich, Michael Hrostoski, Neil Napier, Nicole Seelinger, Raoul Davis, Tal Gur, Taylor Pearson, Till Carlos, Yamile Yemoonyah

Want More?

You can find bonus spreadsheets, audio and video to help you take the work in this book deeper at
www.intuitiveleadershipmastery.com/bonus/

The website also has a blog and podcast.

Happy Intuiting!

45969511R00131

Made in the USA
San Bernardino, CA
22 February 2017